ATARI®
PILOT
FOR BEGINNERS

ATARI®
PILOT
FOR BEGINNERS

Jim Conlan and **Tracy Deliman**
with **Dymax**

RESTON PUBLISHING COMPANY, INC.
A Prentice-Hall Company
RESTON, VIRGINIA 22090

CONTENTS

TO THE READER

In this book you will learn how to give commands to your ATARI* Computer in the PILOT computer language. The PILOT language is designed to do important things quickly and easily. You will learn how to make your ATARI* Computer play music, and display colorful moving pictures, and to do mathematics. You will learn how to use your ATARI* Computer as a thinking tool.

You can read this book even if you don't have a computer. But, to get the most out of this book you should have an ATARI* 400*, or an ATARI* 800* Computer, and the PILOT language cartridge. This book is written to help you get started. Make guesses, experiment, and play around. Have fun.

*Indicates trademark of Atari, Inc. throughout this text.

ATARI®
PILOT
FOR BEGINNERS

THE TURTLE AND THE PILOT

The ATARI* PILOT Language is designed to be quickly learned and easily used. PILOT makes it simple to talk to your ATARI* 400* and ATARI* 800* Computers. PILOT has just the words you need to tell your computer to do fun and interesting things. In this book you will learn how to use the PILOT language. You will learn:

- how to make your computer play and record music you compose
- how to make pictures that move on the screen
- how to make the computer ask questions and check the answers
- how to make the computer tell stories
- how to make the computer do arithmetic
- how to make the computer play games
- how to tell the computer to store and find information for you

THE DOCTOR'S ANSWERING SERVICE

Doctor John Starkweather is a medical doctor. He teaches the art of doctoring at the University of California Medical Center in San Francisco. He saw that

*Indicates trademark of Atari, Inc. throughout this text.

a computer is a useful tool for teaching hard-to-learn medical facts. He thought about how a computer might help. This is what he found.

First of all, the computer can act like a typist and type questions and answers on the screen.

The computer can act like an answering service. A good answering service can accept a message and check the message for special names and numbers.

The computer can act like a calculator and do arithmetic.

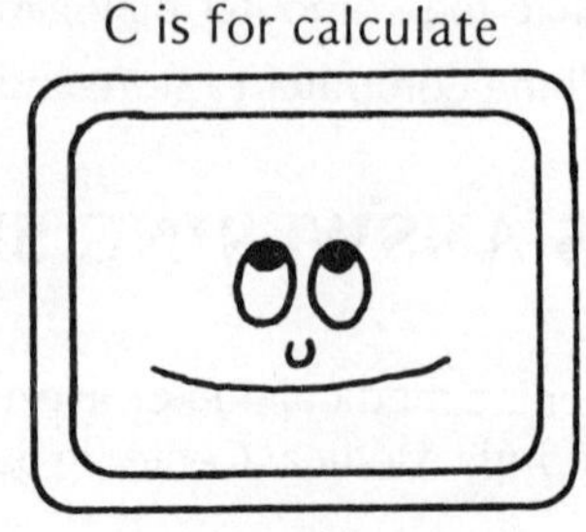

The computer can do lists of tasks that you give it.

Doctor Starkweather's idea was to make the computer act like many different objects. You can tell the typist to type, the answering service to accept messages, the calculator to calculate and the pilot to store lists of directions and tasks and to see that the job is done.

THE TURTLE

Seymour Papert, a scientist at the Massachusetts Institute of Technology (MIT), studies how people learn. He saw that computers can help people learn new things. His book, *Mindstorms*, tells how computers can help people learn to think in new ways. Papert and his co-workers at Massachusetts Institute of Technology developed the turtle. The turtle is a rolling robot with three little wheels, a sensitive bumper around its middle, and a pen that can do drawings. Here is a picture of the turtle:

Cute little devil, isn't it?

If you want to talk to a turtle, you need to know turtle language. You can tell the turtle to go, to turn, and to draw. The turtle can tell you its position. The turtle is very similar to the objects in John Starkweather's computer helper. Why not put all these objects together? That is just what has been done: the ATARI* PILOT Language combines these objects in one system.

THE SOUND MAKER

Here is another object to add to the system. You will certainly want to make some sound. Just tell the sound maker what you want, and it will play your sound.

In the following chapters you will learn how to talk to all of these objects. As you learn about the PILOT language and about your ATARI* Computer, do not feel limited by this book. Skip around, guess, play, take chances, and experiment. You can't hurt the computer. The folks at Atari, Inc. made your computer sturdy, dependable, and forgiving. You will learn the most if you experiment. Make guesses and try them out.

EXPERIMENT, EXPERIMENT, EXPERIMENT

Your computer does even more than this book says. You will find, scattered throughout this book, mysterious computer instructions that are never discussed in detail. Remember that the computer was created by orderly, logical people. There is logic and method hidden everywhere. Be sensitive to both what is said and what is not said.

*Indicates trademark of Atari, Inc. throughout this text.

SELF-TEST ON CHAPTER 1

1. Which of the following objects is in the PILOT language?
   a) the grinch, b) the turtle, c) the kumquat.

2. Which of the following people started the PILOT language?
   a) Thurston Pilot, b) Ada Lovelace, c) John Starkweather.

3. Which word best describes your ATARI* Computer?
   a) sturdy, b) delicate, c) fragile.

4. Which of the following things should you do to learn best?
   a) follow the book exactly, b) experiment on your own, c) don't do
   anything unless told.

5. Which of the following best describes your ATARI* Computer?
   a) impatient and unpredictable, b) disorderly and confused, c) patient
   and orderly.

ANSWERS:

1. b) The turtle is an object in the PILOT language. Turtles like Christmas
   and eat kumquats. The turtle accepts commands and draws on the screen.

2. c) Doctor John Starkweather pioneered in using the computer to help
   people learn. He is one of the inventors of the PILOT language. The
   letters P I L O T stand for the words
   P rogrammed
   I nquiry
   L earning
   O r
   T eaching

3. a) Your ATARI* Computer is sturdy. It will withstand any attack short of
   sledge hammers and dynamite.

*Indicates trademark of Atari, Inc. throughout this text.

4. b) Skip around, try things, and experiment, experiment, experiment; that's the best way to enjoy your ATARI* Computer and learn PILOT.

5. c) One of the nicest things about computers is their patience and orderliness. Your ATARI* Computer was built by logical, orderly people. That is a useful thing to know.

*Indicates trademark of Atari, Inc. throughout this text.

THE KEYBOARD

Your ATARI* Computer has an editor to help you print things on the screen. In this chapter you will learn:

- how to use the MEMO PAD editor
- how to control the position of the cursor
- how to print anyplace on the screen
- how to erase mistakes
- how to clear the screen
- how to make pictures on the screen using letters
- how to make pictures using ATARI* Computer graphic characters
- how to write and decode secret messages written in graphic code
- how to reverse light and dark in the letters you type
- how to play Fuji roulette

HOW TO FLY WITHOUT A PILOT

It's time to fly. Is everything ready? Plug in the plug, and hook up the television.

*Indicates trademark of Atari, Inc. throughout this text.

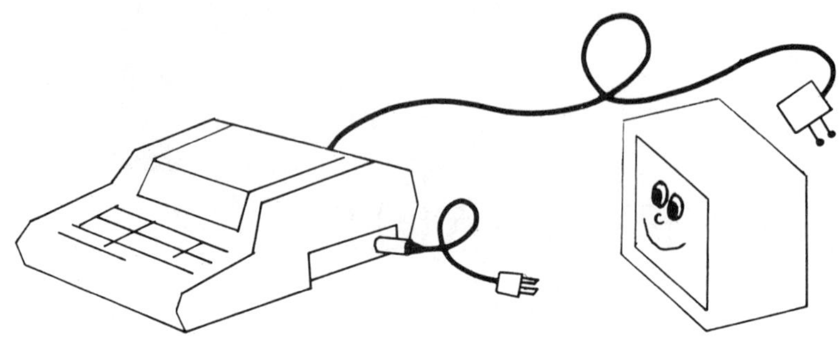

Start with an empty computer. Open the top.

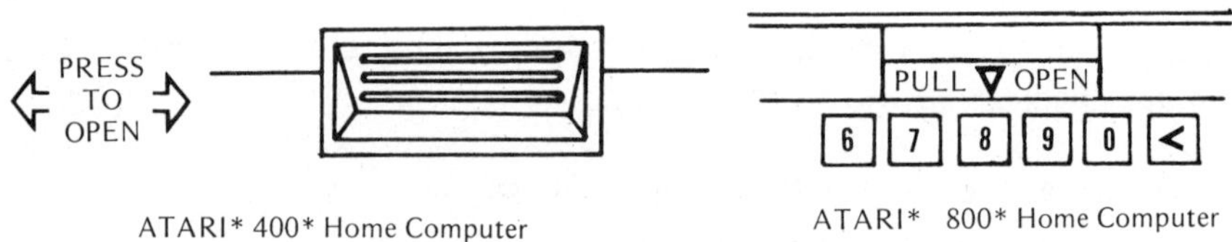

ATARI* 400* Home Computer

ATARI* 800* Home Computer

When you open the top, here is what you see:

ATARI* 800* Home Computer

ATARI* 400* Home Computer

You will see how the computer works with its personality gone. Take out any cartridge in the cartridge slot. Is the slot empty? Good. Now the computer works in the simplest way.

It's simpler with the motor out

Close the top firmly. The top needs to be closed all the way before the computer will work. Now, turn on the TV, and turn on the computer using the on/off switch on the right side. Here is what you see on the screen:

ATARI* Computer MEMO PAD

When no cartridge is in the slot, the ATARI* Computer functions as a MEMO PAD. The computer is an editor to help you get your message onto the screen. You can leave messages, reminders, or doodles. Give it a try.
Type in

FOOL AROUND, FIDDLE, DIDDLE, AND DOODLE.

What do you suppose all those fancy keys are for? Try them. You can't hurt the computer. Experiment. Later when you put the PILOT cartridge back in, these keys will still work in the same way they do now.

*Indicates trademark of Atari, Inc. throughout this text.

THE CURSOR

The white square that moves on the screen as you type is called the CURSOR. The cursor shows you where you are about to type.

THE ARROW KEYS

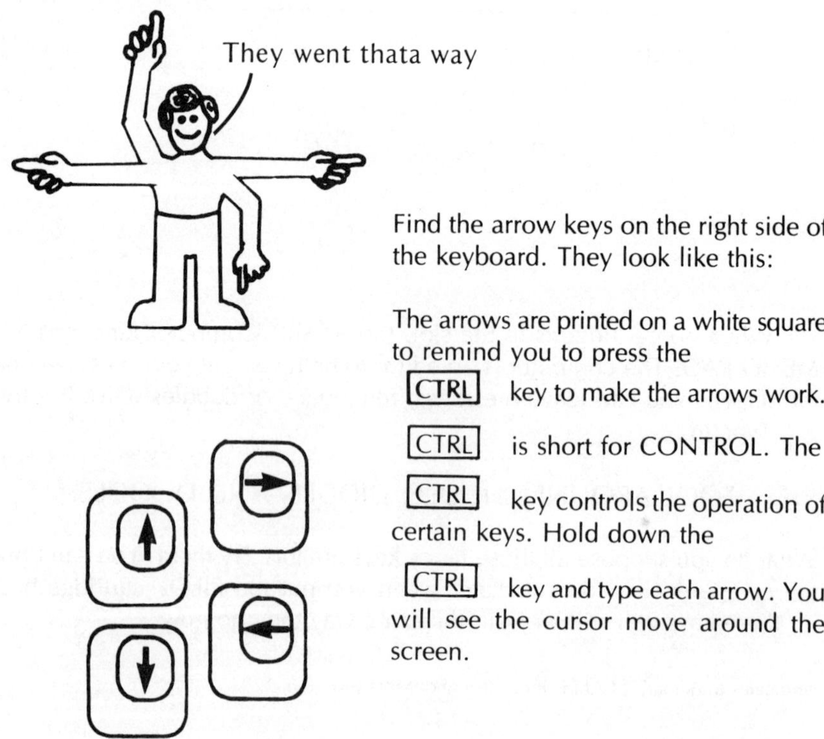

Find the arrow keys on the right side of the keyboard. They look like this:

The arrows are printed on a white square to remind you to press the [CTRL] key to make the arrows work.

[CTRL] is short for CONTROL. The [CTRL] key controls the operation of certain keys. Hold down the [CTRL] key and type each arrow. You will see the cursor move around the screen.

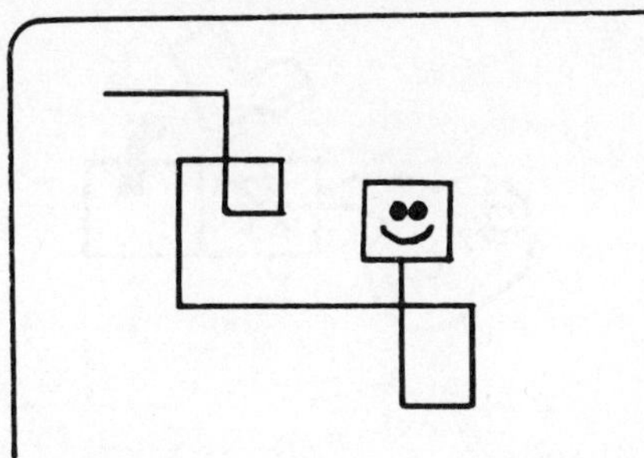

The arrows are called the CURSOR CONTROL ARROWS. The cursor control arrows allow you to type anyplace on the screen.

Type this:

A B C D E

Now use the cursor control arrows and the long space bar to blank out the B and the D. The screen should look like this:

A C E

THE DELETE/BACK S KEY

The [DELETE/BACK S] key is the most wonderful key of all. It is only human to make mistrakes. If you make an error, you can erase the error with the [DELETE/BACK S] key. It is on the top row, right side and looks like this:

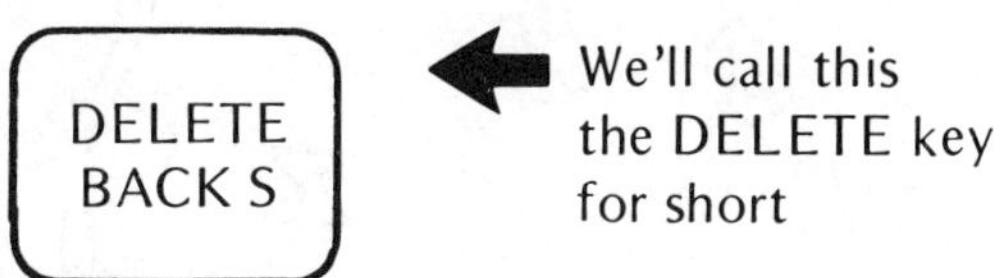

Type this:

A B C

Now press the [DELETE] key. Each time you press the [DELETE] key the cursor hops back one space and blanks out whatever was there.

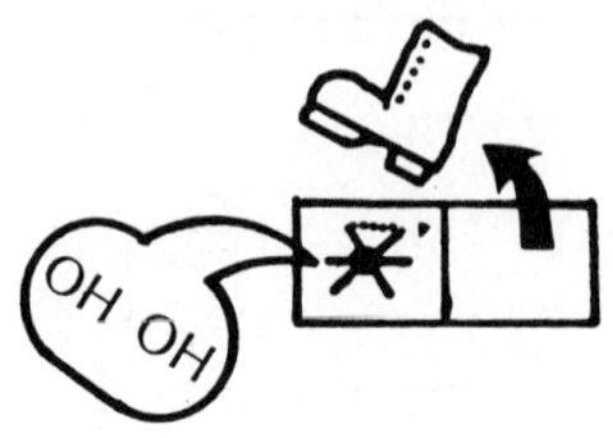

THE CLEAR KEY

When the screen begins to fill with useless litter, clutter, and junk, you need the [CLEAR] key. The [CLEAR] key cleans the screen. The [CLEAR] key is on the right side in the top row. It looks like this:

Do some messing around. You will need some clutter and junk to clean up.

Are you ready for some screen cleaning?
Hold the [SHIFT] key down and press the [CLEAR] key.

FLASH! ZIP!

The screen is clear and clean.

MAKING PICTURES

Now that you can move the cursor and erase characters, you can compose pictures on the screen. Here are some examples:

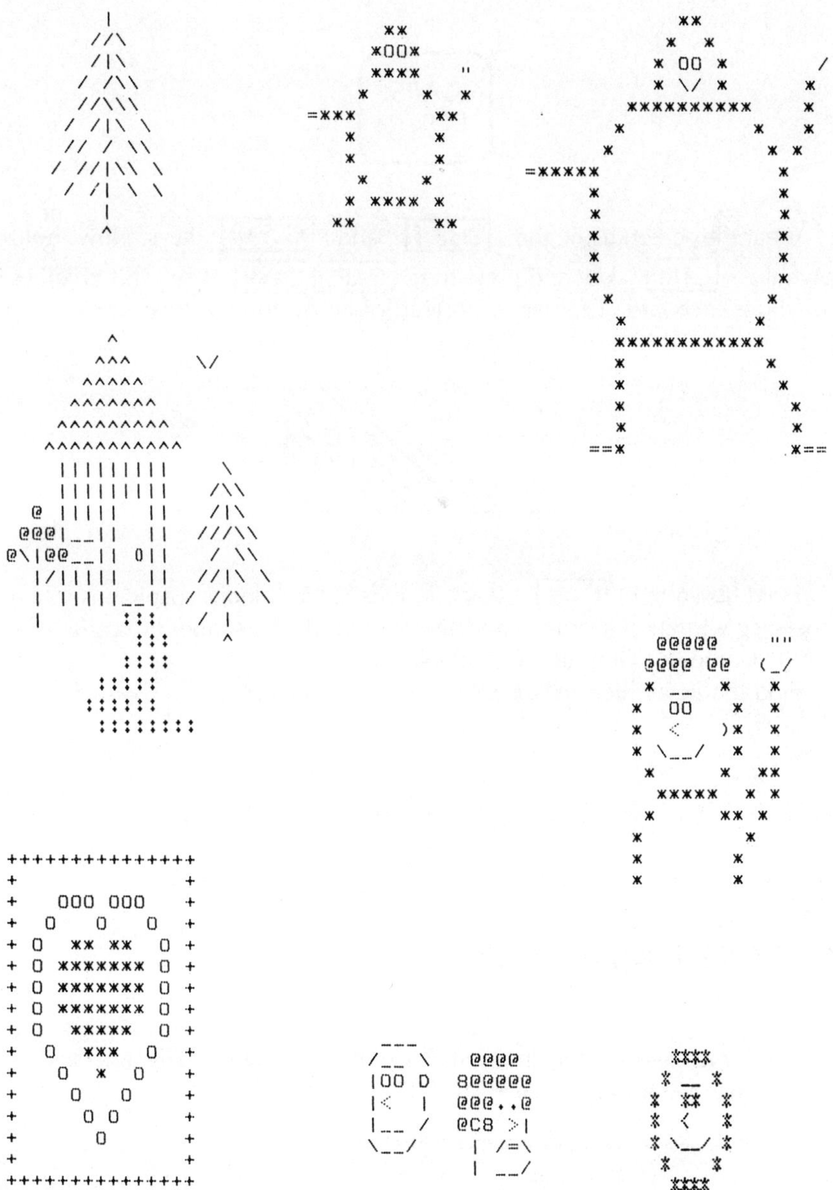

MORE DRAWING TOOLS

Your ATARI* Computer has other shapes you can type besides ordinary letters and numbers. Find the CAPS/LOWR key on the right side of the keyboard. It looks like this:

CAPS
LOWR

Clear the screen using the SHIFT and CLEAR keys. Now, hold down the CTRL key and press the CAPS/LOWR key. This changes the whole keyboard. Type an A. Instead of an A, you see this:

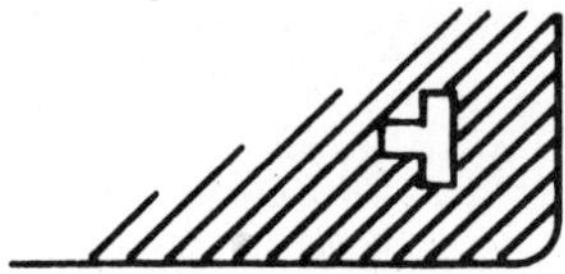

Hold down the CTRL key and type CAT. It looks suspiciously like a message written in a strange and secret code. These shapes are called the ATARI* Computer Graphic Characters.

Find the key which makes this graphic character:

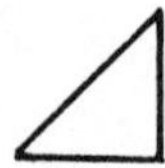

A SECRET MESSAGE

Here is a message written in ATARI* Computer Graphic Characters. Can you discover what the message says?

*Indicates trademark of Atari, Inc. throughout this text.

CONTROL KEY GRAPHICS

If you hold the   CTRL   key down while you type a key, the key makes a graphic shape instead of a letter. Here is a picture of the keyboard with the graphic shapes on the keys:

Use the graphic shapes on the keys   CTRL   Q, W, E, A, S, D, Z, X, and C to make a design like this:

Use the graphic shapes to print a rocket on the bottom of the screen, like this:

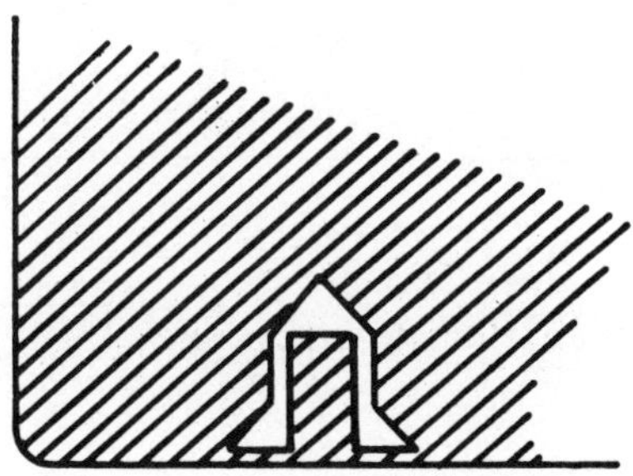

Now, press the [RETURN] key. If you keep pressing the [RETURN] key, the rocket will rise and move off the top of the screen.

UNLOCKING THE KEYBOARD

When you press the [CAPS/LOWR] key the keyboard locks or unlocks. The [CAPS/LOWR] key might as well be called the [LOCK/UNLOCK] key. Press the [CAPS/LOWR] key. Now, the keyboard is unlocked. That means it types in the normal way. Type this:

[A][B][C]

You see this:

a b c

Hold down the [SHIFT] key and type this:

[A][B][C]

Now you see this:

ABC

The [SHIFT] key makes capital, or upper case, letters. Hold down the [SHIFT] key and type the [CAPS/LOWR] key. Now the [SHIFT] key is locked on. The keyboard just types capital letters now. Type this:

[A][B][C]

You see:

ABC

Type the [CAPS/LOWR] key to unlock the [SHIFT] key. Type again:

[A][B][C]

You see:

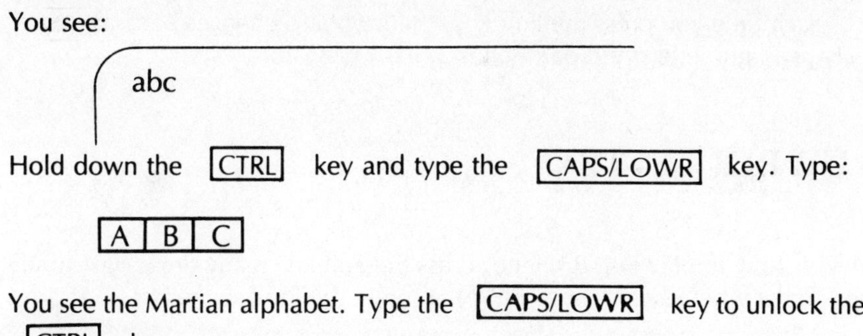

Hold down the CTRL key and type the CAPS/LOWR key. Type:

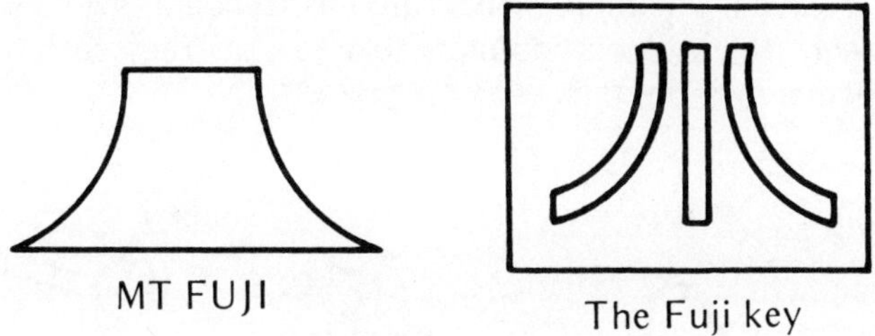

You see the Martian alphabet. Type the CAPS/LOWR key to unlock the CTRL key.

THE FUJI KEY

Do you see that odd-looking key at the lower right corner of the keyboard? It looks like Mount Fuji, so we call it the Fuji key.

MT FUJI

The Fuji key

Clear the screen. Now, type this:

The keyboard has changed. Light and dark are reversed on each letter you type. You see this:

← Dark letters on a light background

Each time you press the Fuji key, the keyboard changes back and forth between light letters and dark letters.

FUJI ROULETTE

Here is how to play Fuji Roulette. Press the Fuji key many times, fast, until you forget whether it is on or off. Now press the long space bar.

☐ means **BANG!**.

Good luck.

SOME HELPERS

There are three friendly helpers at work when you type a key and print a letter on the screen. The three helpers are the keyboard, the screen editor, and the screen. These objects do more than just sit. They each have some special jobs that they do.

When you type a key, the keyboard sends a message to the screen editor. The message tells the screen editor what key you pressed. The screen editor decides what to do with the message. Some keys tell the screen editor to do a task.

Hold down the SHIFT key, and type the CLEAR key. The keyboard treats this as a single key. It sends a special mark ↰ to the screen editor. The SHIFT CLEAR mark is a little curved arrow.

The screen editor doesn't print the special curved arrow. The screen editor does a task instead. It wipes the screen clear. If you'd like to allow the screen editor to escape its screen cleaning task, then try this:

Type the escape key   ESC   on the upper left side of the keyboard.

Now type   SHIFT   CLEAR   . You see something new on the screen:

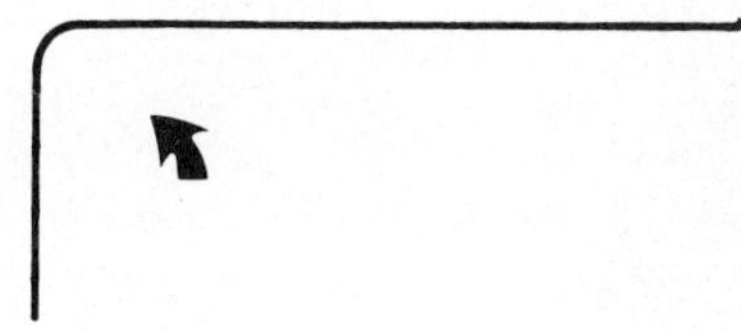

The escape key   ESC   tells the screen editor to take a short vacation from its job. The screen editor sends the curved arrow mark   ↰   straight onto the screen. The curved arrow   ↰   is the   SHIFT   CLEAR   mark.

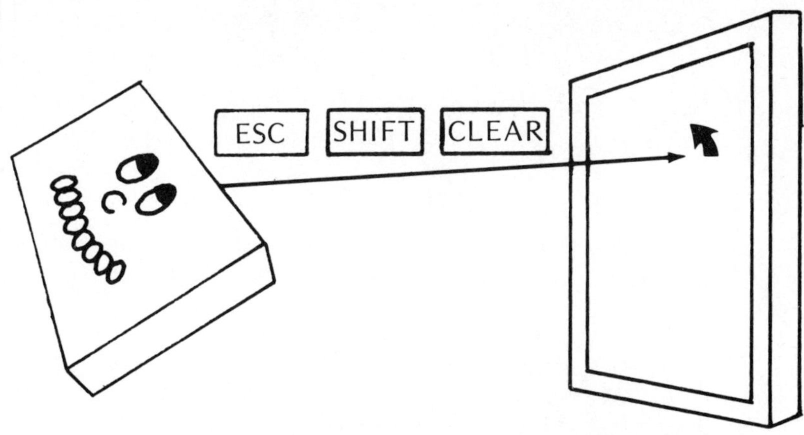

THE ESC KEY ESCAPES THE SCREEN EDITOR

The cursor control arrows can be made to print arrows on the screen. Try these:

ESC	CTRL	(→)
ESC	CTRL	(↑)
ESC	CTRL	(←)
ESC	CTRL	(↓)

SELF-TEST ON CHAPTER 2

Mark each of the following sentences true or false:

1. The ATARI* Computer can work without a cartridge in the slot.
2. The ATARI* Computer can function as a memo pad.
3. You can't hurt the computer by typing any of its keys.
4. The name of the white square that shows where you are typing is called the frammis.
5. The Fuji key deletes mistakes.
6. Each key can make more than one kind of mark.
7. The $\boxed{\text{SHIFT}}$ $\boxed{\text{CLEAR}}$ key wipes the screen clean.
8. The ATARI* Computer can only print letters and numbers.
9. Holding down the $\boxed{\text{CTRL}}$ key affects the mark that the key makes.
10. There is a screen editor that checks what you type.

ANSWERS:

1. True. The ATARI* Computer works as a memo pad when the cartridge is not in the slot.
2. True. The ATARI* Computer serves as a memo pad. The computer also serves as an editor to help you write on the screen.
3. True. You can't hurt the computer by anything you type. Experiment all you want.
4. False. The white square is not called a frammis. The white square that tells you where you are on the screen is called the cursor.
5. False. The Fuji key doesn't delete mistakes. The Fuji key causes the keyboard to reverse light and dark when it prints letters and shapes on the screen.

6. True. Each key can make many different shapes. The SHIFT key, the CTRL key and the Fuji key affect what each key will type.

7. True. The SHIFT   CLEAR key clears the screen.

8. False. The ATARI* Computer can print 32 different graphic shapes. Holding down the CTRL key makes the keys print the graphic shapes.

9. True. The CTRL key makes the control arrows work and makes the graphic shapes appear.

10. True. The ATARI* Computer has a screen editor that helps you print on the screen. The screen editor can clear the screen, move the cursor, and insert or delete letters and shapes on the screen.

SUMMARY OF CHAPTER 2

In this chapter you learned:

- how to open the top of the computer
- that the computer serves as a memo pad
- that the cursor shows where you are typing
- that the CTRL key makes the cursor control arrows work
- that the BACK S key hops back one space and deletes a letter
- that the SHIFT   CLEAR key clears the screen
- that the CTRL key makes the keys print control key graphic shapes
- that the Fuji key causes dark and light to reverse in letters
- that the keyboard sends letters to the screen editor, and the screen editor either does a task or sends the letter to the screen
- that the ESC key causes the letters to bypass the screen editor

*Indicates trademark of Atari, Inc. throughout this text.

3

GETTING STARTED

In this chapter you will learn:

- how to insert the PILOT cartridge in its slot
- how to tell the computer to type words on the screen
- that the ATARI* Computer can make thirty-two sounds
- how to tell the computer to turn sounds on and off
- how the sounds are related to the piano keyboard
- that numbered commands are saved by the computer
- how to RUN lists of commands
- how to tell the computer to pause for a period of time
- that the command NEW clears out old programs
- how to make the computer play melodies that you compose
- that the ATARI* Computer can play up to four sounds at once
- how to use the
  CTRL   INSERT   and   CTRL   DELETE   keys

THE PILOT COMES ABOARD

It is time to put the PILOT cartridge into the computer. The cartridge gives
the computer its personality. Open the top of your ATARI* Computer. On

*Indicates trademark of Atari, Inc. throughout this text.

the ATARI* 400* Computer you see one slot for a cartridge. On the ATARI* 800* Computer you see two slots. The left one is where the PILOT cartridge goes.

The cartridge only goes in one way. You can't put it in wrong. Wiggle it firmly down into place. There, it fits just perfectly.

Close the top firmly. Turn on the computer, and then the TV. Here is what you see:

```
ATARI PILOT (C) COPYRIGHT 1980
READY
```

*Indicates trademark of Atari, Inc. throughout this text.

The computer is ready to listen to your commands. It is easy to talk to your computer. It speaks a very simple language. The PILOT language has only a few words in it. That's good, and that's bad. The good news is that you don't need to learn many words to talk to the computer. The bad news is that the computer can't understand many words.

Type this:

Now press the big [RETURN] key on right side of the keyboard. You see this on the screen:

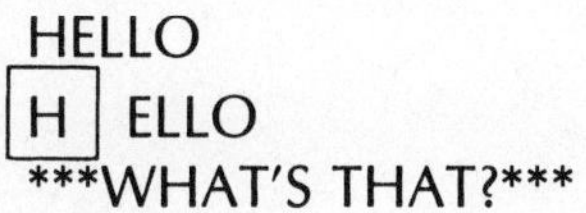

The computer doesn't understand the word HELLO. When the computer doesn't understand what you say, it prints your message out again followed by the words ***WHAT'S THAT?***

THE TYPE COMMAND T:

You can tell the computer to type messages on the screen. Here is how you do it.

Type this just as it appears:

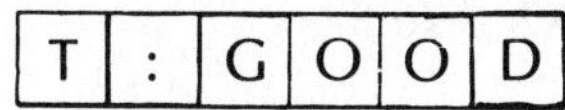

Now press the [RETURN] key. You see this:

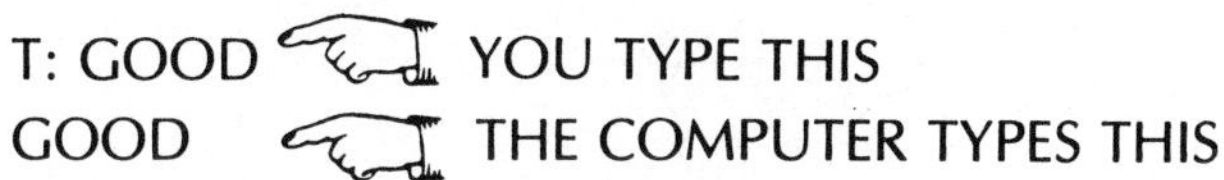

The computer knows that T: is a command to type whatever comes next. When you press the [RETURN] key, the computer does what it was told and types out GOOD on the screen.

THE RETURN KEY

The [RETURN] key is the signal to the computer that you are done typing. The computer knows that you are done typing a line when you press the [RETURN] key.

Use the command T: to make the computer type your name.

T: NURDLE FERGELBURP   [RETURN]

The [RETURN] key also sends the cursor down to the beginning of the next line. What happens if the cursor is at the bottom of the screen and there is no next line? The clever computer screen shifts everything on the screen upwards to make room. Try this:

Type [SHIFT]   [CLEAR] to clear the screen. Now press the [RETURN] key again and again, until the cursor is at the beginning of the bottom line. Now fill the line with A's, like this:

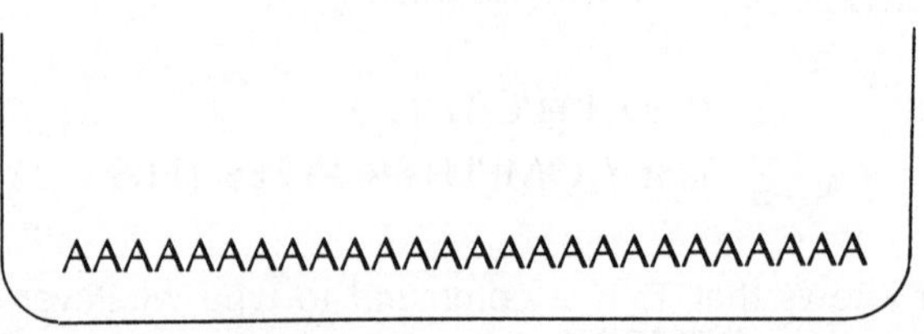

Now press [RETURN] a few times. The line of A's moves up the screen.

THE SOUND COMMAND SO:

Your ATARI* Computer is able to make sounds. Your computer can make thirty-two different sounds. Here is the way you tell the computer to turn on a sound:

Type this:

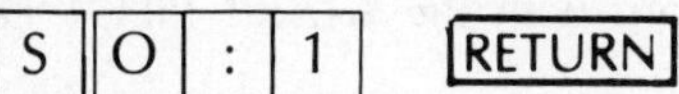

You hear a low hum. The low hum is sound number 1.

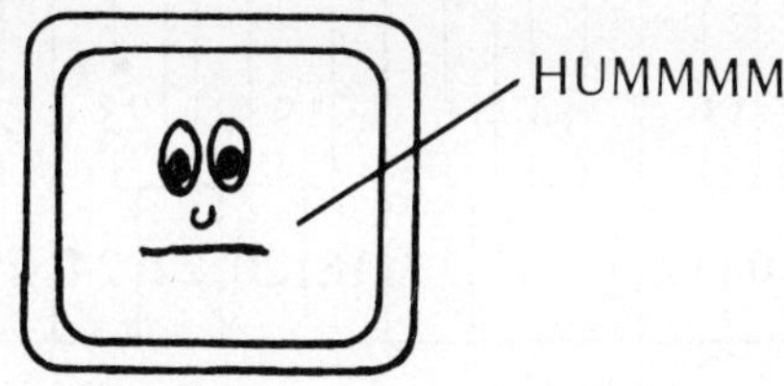

Type this:

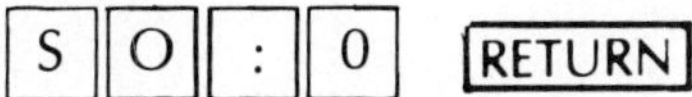

The sound turns off. SO: is no sound at all.
Type this:

This also turns off the sound.
Type this:

This is the highest sound your computer plays.

SO:	this is the sound of silence.
SO: 0	this is also silent.
SO: 1	this is the lowest sound.
SO: 31	this is the highest sound.

*Indicates trademark of Atari, Inc. throughout this text.

Type this:

SO: 7   [RETURN]

Find the [BREAK] key on the upper right corner of the keyboard. Now press the [BREAK] key. The [BREAK] key also stops the sound.

The sounds that your computer makes are like the sounds a piano plays. Here is a picture of a piano keyboard with the ATARI* PILOT Language sound numbers on each key:

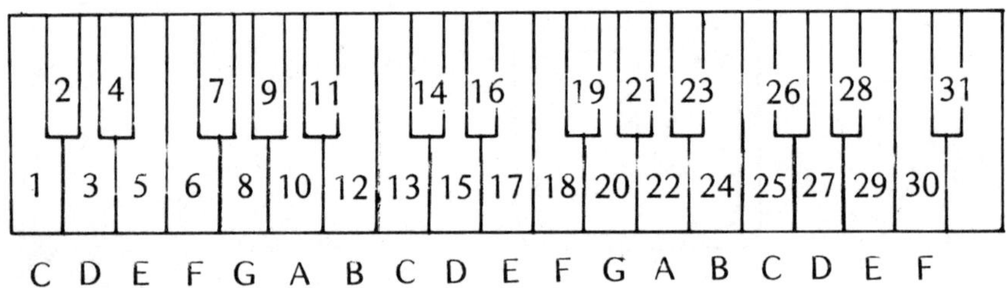

Here are the sound numbers for the DO, RE, MI scale:

DO	SO: 13
RE	SO: 15
MI	SO: 17
FA	SO: 18
SO	SO: 20
LA	SO: 22
SI	SO: 24
DO	SO: 25

STORING LISTS OF COMMANDS

There is a way to store lists of commands in the computer. When the computer finds a line that starts with a number, it doesn't immediately perform the command on the line, but instead stores the line away in its memory.

Type these two lines, numbers and all.

1 T: THIS | RETURN | ☜ THE COMPUTER STORES
                                    NUMBERED LINES

2 T: IS | RETURN |

The computer doesn't type the word THIS or the word IS. Instead, the computer stores the list of two commands away in its memory. The list of commands is stored even if you clear the screen.

Type this to clear the screen:

| SHIFT | | CLEAR |

This clears the screen, but the list is still stored in the computer's memory. You can get the list back again.

Type this to see the list of stored commands:

| L | I | S | T | | RETURN |

You see this:

1 T: THIS
2 T: IS

The computer got the list from its memory and printed it on the screen.

RUN COMPUTER RUN

Whenever you are ready, the computer will run through your list of stored commands and perform each of them. Type | SHIFT | | CLEAR | to clear the screen, and then type this:

| R | U | N | | RETURN |

You see this:

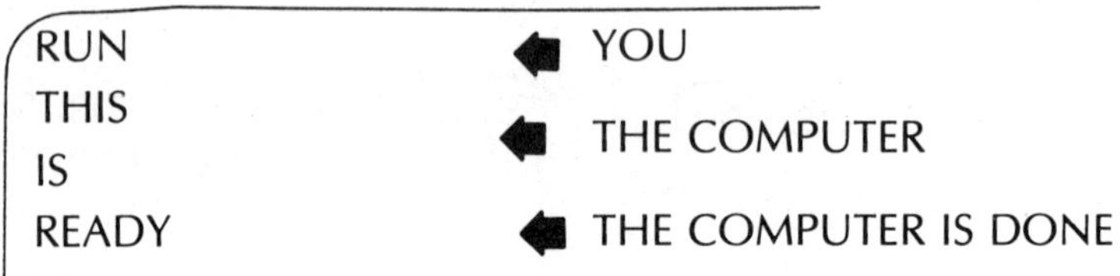

The computer got the list of stored commands and performed them one at a time. Here is the list of commands again:

```
1 T: THIS
2 T: IS
```

Line 1 tells the computer to type the word THIS. The computer types THIS, and then goes on to line 2. Line 2 tell the computer to type IS. The computer types IS, and then goes to the next line. Since there is nothing to do, the computer types READY and stops.

A SHORT PAUSE

The computer is exceedingly quick. Sometimes you will want to tell it to pause for a moment before going on. The command to tell the computer to pause looks like this:

```
PA:60
```

This command tells the computer to pause for 60 jiffies. It takes 60 jiffies to make 1 second.

Clear the screen by typing

SHIFT   CLEAR

Now, type these lines:

```
3 PA: 60     PAUSE 60 JIFFIES (1 SECOND)
4 T: THE END     TYPE "THE END"
```

Remember to type the [RETURN] key at the end of each line.
Now, list the program. Type

LIST ☞ REMEMBER TO PRESS [RETURN]

You see the whole list of commands:

    1 T: THIS
    2 T: IS
    3 PA: 60
    4 T: THE END

A list of commands is called a PROGRAM. You have just written a program.
It is time to RUN the program.
    Type

RUN [RETURN]

You see this:

    RUN
    THIS
    IS

The computer pauses for 1 second, and then the last line appears:

    THE END

    Type:

    [SHIFT] [CLEAR]

Now, type this new line 3:

    3 PA: 600 [RETURN]

    Type:

RUN [RETURN]

You will have to wait a little while for the last line to appear.

Here is a table that tells how long pauses are in seconds:

```
PA:1       1/60 SECOND
PA:60         1 SECOND
PA:120        2 SECONDS
PA:180        3 SECONDS
PA:240        4 SECONDS
PA:300        5 SECONDS
PA:360        6 SECONDS
PA:420        7 SECONDS
PA:480        8 SECONDS
PA:540        9 SECONDS
PA:600       10 SECONDS

PA:3600    1 MINUTE
PA:7200    2 MINUTES
PA:10800   3 MINUTES
```

A NEW PROGRAM

Are you ready for a new program? Then type this:

N E W   RETURN

This command tells the computer that you are done with the old program. The computer prepares for your new program by clearing the old program out of its memory. You can check that the old list is gone. Type this:

LIST   RETURN

You see this:

LIST   YOU TYPE THIS
READY   THE COMPUTER TYPES THIS

The old list is completely gone.

A SHORT MELODY

You can use the pause command to make a melody that can be stored and run. Here's an example to try. Remember to press the   RETURN   key at the end of each line.

```
100 *MELODY        THIS PROGRAM HAS A NAME
110 SO: 1
120 PA: 10
130 SO: 8
140 PA: 20
150 SO:17
160 PA: 30
170 SO: 5
180 PA: 20
190 SO: 8
200 PA: 30
```

Now, type

RUN   [RETURN]

Do you recognize the tune? You can RUN this program as many times as you like. It never wears out.

Add a new line to the program. Type this:

210 J: *MELODY   [RETURN]

The command J: *MELODY tells the computer to jump up to the top of the program to the line labeled *MELODY. We'll talk more about jumping later. Now, hear the result. Type

RUN   [RETURN]

The tune now plays over and over again. When you have heard enough, press

[BREAK]

MORE VOICES

You can play more than one sound at a time. Type this:

SO: 1, 8   [RETURN]

You hear sounds 1 and 8 played together.
You can play three sounds together. Type this:

SO: 1, 13, 25   [RETURN]

You can play four sounds together. Type this:

SO: 1, 5, 8, 13   [RETURN]

Here is our candidate for the worst possible sound combinations:

SO: 21, 23, 24

Can you do worse than that?

MUSIC FOR A MONSTER MOVIE

You've noticed that some sounds are terrible together, like music in a monster movie. Try this. You'll hate it.

```
100 *MONSTER
110 SO: 7, 8
120 PA: 120
130 SO: 6, 8
140 PA: 60
150 SO: 9, 10
160 PA: 180
170 SO: 9, 12, 13
180 PA: 120
190 J: *MONSTER
```

190 J: *MONSTER   JUMP BACK TO *MONSTER

Can you make spookier music than that? Give it a try. Type LIST [RETURN] to get a copy of the previous program on the screen. Now, use the control arrows to change the numbers in the program. Remember to press [RETURN] after you change a line. When you press [RETURN] the computer will enter your changed line in the list.

SPACE FOR YOUR MONSTER MUSIC

MUSIC APPRECIATION TEST

Which sounds go together well? Try these pairs of sounds, and circle the word that you feel applies to the sound combination:

```
SO: 1, 2  GOOD BAD
SO: 1, 3  GOOD BAD
SO: 1, 4  GOOD BAD
SO: 1, 5  GOOD BAD
SO: 1, 6  GOOD BAD
SO: 1, 7  GOOD BAD
SO: 1, 8  GOOD BAD
SO: 1, 9  GOOD BAD
SO: 1, 10 GOOD BAD
SO: 1, 11 GOOD BAD
SO: 1, 12 GOOD BAD
SO: 1, 13 GOOD BAD
```

The philosopher Pythagoras lived 2500 years ago. He thought that sounds 1 and 8 were especially pleasing. Do you agree? Musicians over the centuries have searched for sounds that go well together. Some people think that sounds 1, 5, and 8 are very pleasing. Give it a try:

$$SO: 1, 5, 8$$

Do you like it? Notice that 5 is 4 larger than 1, and 8 is 7 larger than 1. The traditional rule for making 3 sounds that go together is this:

- ■ Choose a first sound number
- ■ Add 4 to the first number to get the second sound number
- ■ Add 7 to the first number to get the third sound number

If 2 is the first sound number, what is the second number? ________ What is the third number? ________ Did you get 6 and 9? How does it sound? Try it:

SO: 2, 6, 9

PHANTOM NOTES

When you play two sounds together, a mysterious thing happens. Two new sounds are created which are different from either of the original sounds. One new sound is lower than either sound; one new sound is higher than either sound. These new sounds are called BEAT notes.
Try this:

SO: 1, 2

Can you hear a faint, wobbly low note? The high-beat note is difficult to hear. It is a weak sound like SO: 13 or SO: 14.

INSERTING AND DELETING

There are two keys that you will use a lot. You may have already discovered these useful keys. Find the [INSERT] key on the top right side of the keyboard. It looks like this:

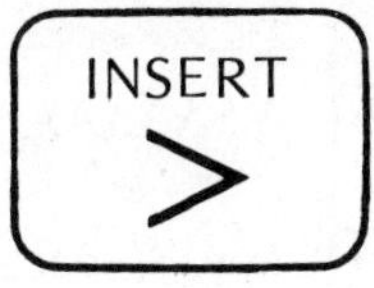

Type [SHIFT] [CLEAR] to clear the screen. Now type

A B

Use the control arrows to move the cursor over the letter B:

A [B]

Now, hold the [CTRL] key down, and type the [INSERT] key. The B scoots over to the right, leaving a space. The cursor is still in the same position, right after the A.

A [ ] B

Press the [CTRL] [INSERT] key a few more times. What happens? Every time you press the [CTRL] [INSERT] key, more spaces are inserted, and the B is moved to the right. The cursor stays put.

It is time for the [CTRL] [DELETE] key to do something. Hold down the [CTRL] key, and type the [DELETE] key. Now the cursor eats up those spaces. Chomp, chomp, chomp. Here comes the B.

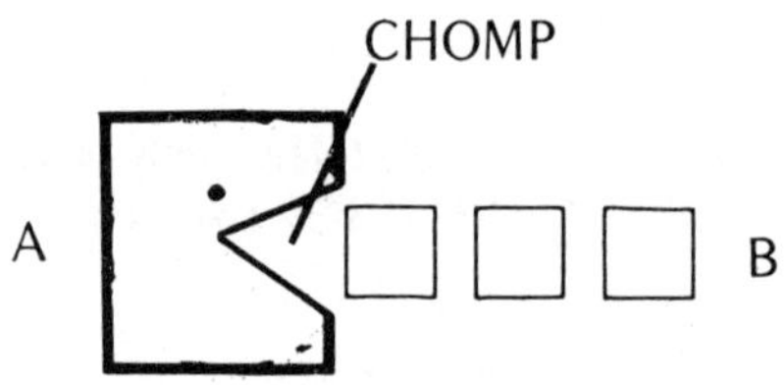

Fill a line with A's like this:

AAAAAAAAAAAAAAAAAAAAAAAAAA

Now use the control arrows to move the cursor to the middle of the line like this:

AAAAAAAAAA [A] AAAAAAAAAAAA

Type the [CTRL] [INSERT] key. A space is inserted, and the A's move right a notch.

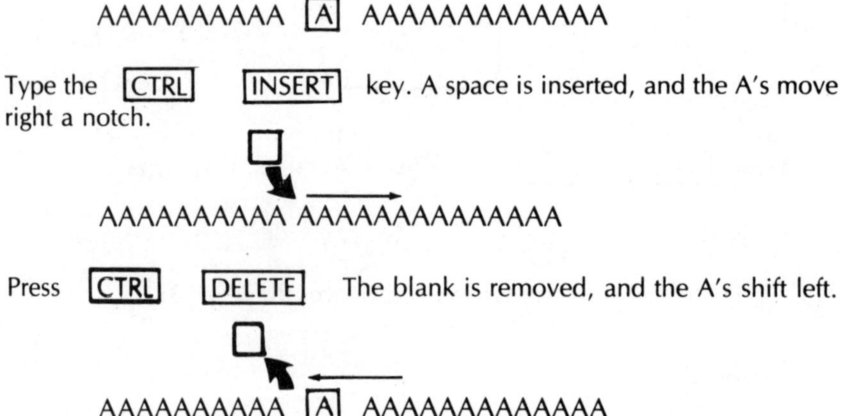

Press [CTRL] [DELETE]   The blank is removed, and the A's shift left.

AAAAAAAAAA [A] AAAAAAAAAAAA

SELF-TEST ON CHAPTER **3**

1. Tell what each of these commands do:

   T: WHAT _________________________________
   SO: 1 _________________________________
   PA: 60 _____________________________
   SO: 1, 8 ___________________________

2. What command will turn off the sound? _______

3. How many sounds can the computer play at once? _______

4. The command PA: 60 will cause a pause of how long? _______

5. Write a program that turns on sound 1 for 1 second, then turns it off.

   10 ________________________________
   20 ________________________________
   30 ________________________________

6. What do you type to tell the computer to perform a stored program? _______

7. What key(s) do you use to make room for another word in a line? _______

8. What do you type to see the program list? _______

9. What do you type to clear out the old program from the computer's memory? _______

10. Write a program that types START, waits 10 seconds, then types STOP, and stops.

    10 ________________________________
    20 ________________________________
    30 ________________________________

ANSWERS:

1. T: WHAT tells the computer to type the word WHAT.

    SO: 1 tells the computer to turn on sound 1.
    PA: 60 tells the computer to pause for 60 jiffies, or 1 second.
    SO: 1, 8 tells the computer to turn on sounds 1 and 8.

2. The command SO: will turn off the sound. The command SO: 0 will also turn off the sound. The break key will also turn off the sound.

3. The computer can play four sounds at once.

4. The command PA: 60 will make the computer pause for 1 second.

5. Here is one program that works:

        10 SO: 1
        20 PA: 60
        30 SO:

6. You type RUN to tell the computer to perform a stored program.

7. The CTRL   INSERT key makes room in a line by inserting spaces in the line.

8. To see a stored program list, you type LIST.

9. To clear an old program out of the computer's memory, you type NEW.

10. Here is one program that works:

        10 T: START
        20 PA: 60
        30 T: STOP

SUMMARY OF CHAPTER 3

In this chapter you learned:

- how to insert the PILOT cartridge in its slot
- that the computer can only understand a few simple words
- that the computer types ***WHAT'S THAT?*** when it doesn't understand
- that T: tells the computer to type
- that the [RETURN] key tells the computer you are done with a line
- that the command SO: tells the computer to turn on the sound
- that the computer can make thirty-two sounds
- that the sounds the computer makes are related to piano keys
- that a command preceded by a number is stored
- that the command LIST causes the computer to print the list of stored commands
- that the command RUN causes the computer to perform the list of stored commands
- that a list of stored commands is called a PROGRAM
- that the command PA: is used to tell the computer to pause
- that the command NEW clears old programs out of the computer's memory
- that four sounds can be played at the same time
- that the [CTRL] [INSERT] key makes space in a line by inserting spaces and shifting letters to the right
- that the [CTRL] [DELETE] key removes letters and shifts the remaining letters left to fill the space

MEET THE GRAPHICS TURTLE

4

In this chapter you will learn:

- that your computer has an invisible graphics turtle
- that you can give the graphics turtle commands
- that the turtle can GO some number of steps, DRAW some number of steps, and TURN some number of degrees
- how to quickly draw triangles, squares, circles, and other figures on the screen
- how to make your drawings appear to move
- how to make the computer choose a number for you
- how to draw in RED, YELLOW, or BLUE
- how to erase lines

GROVER THE GRAPHICS TURTLE

The PILOT language is designed so that you can easily draw on the screen. The graphics commands allow you to tell an invisible turtle to move on the screen and draw. It is remarkably easy to talk to the turtle.

Start fresh. Turn off the computer and then turn it on again. You see this message on the screen:

```
ATARI PILOT (C) COPYRIGHT ATARI 1980
READY
```

Everything is ready to go. The invisible turtle is waiting for your commands. Here is a picture of the turtle in the middle of the screen.

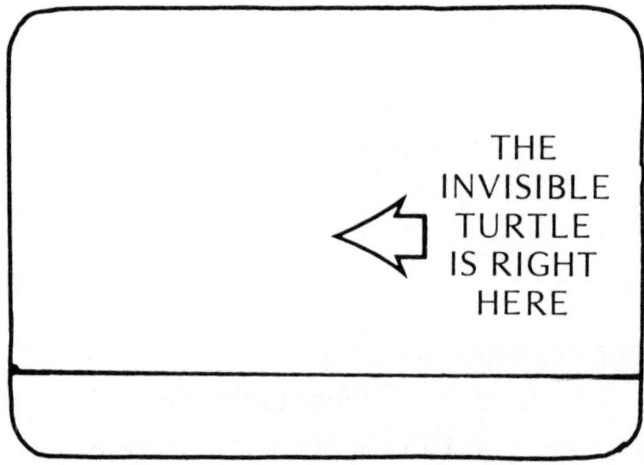

Since invisible turtles are so hard to keep track of, we will draw a picture of the turtle. You'll have to imagine the turtle on your screen. The turtle starts in the middle of the screen, pointed up.

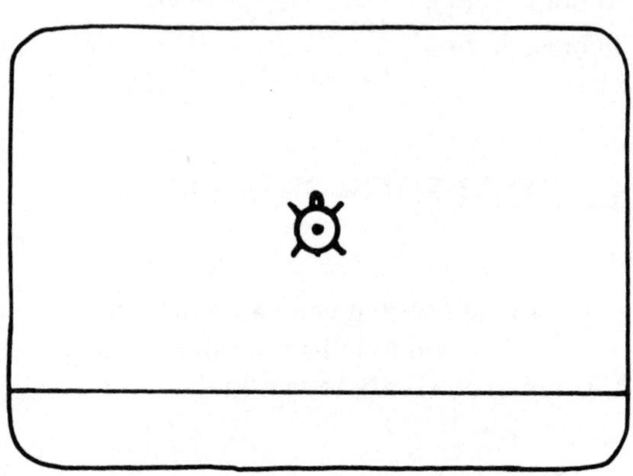

All commands to Grover the graphics turtle are preceded by GR:. Some people say this stands for GRAPHICS, but we know that it stands for GROVER.

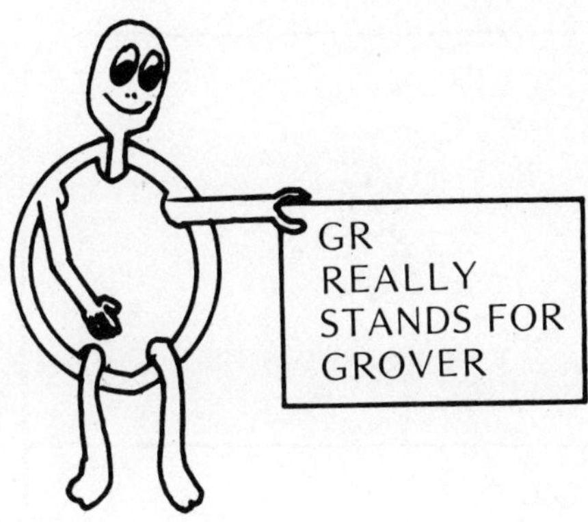

Here is the command that tells Grover to go 0 steps and make a mark. Type this:

GR: GO 0   RETURN

This is what you see:

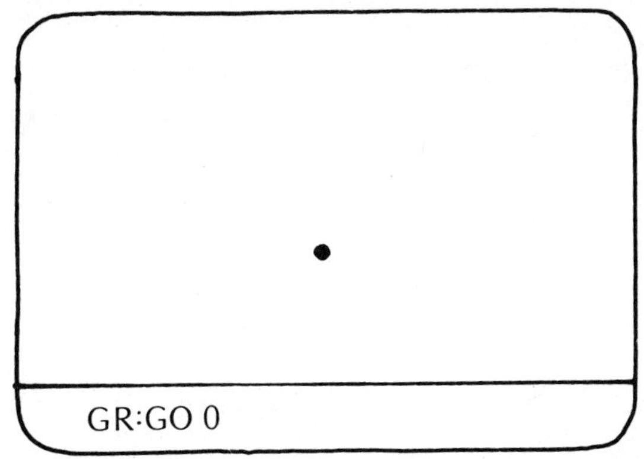

Let's tell the turtle to take a short trip. Type this:

GR: GO 6   RETURN

This is a very obedient turtle. It moves ahead 6 steps and makes a mark. Here is what you see (if you imagine the invisible turtle).

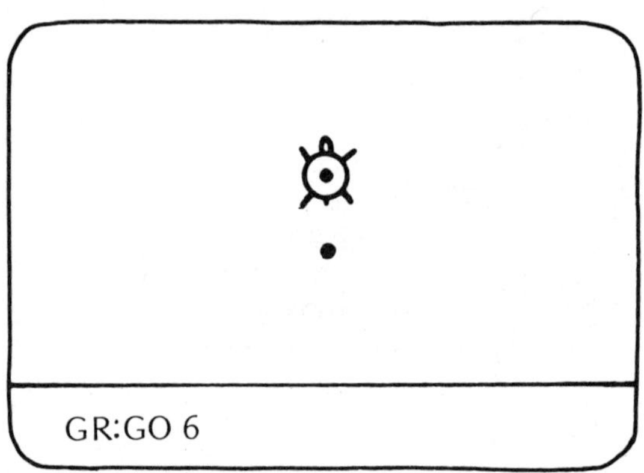

Give the same command again. Type:

GR: GO 6   REMEMBER TO PRESS   RETURN

You see just what you might have expected to see, another yellow dot.

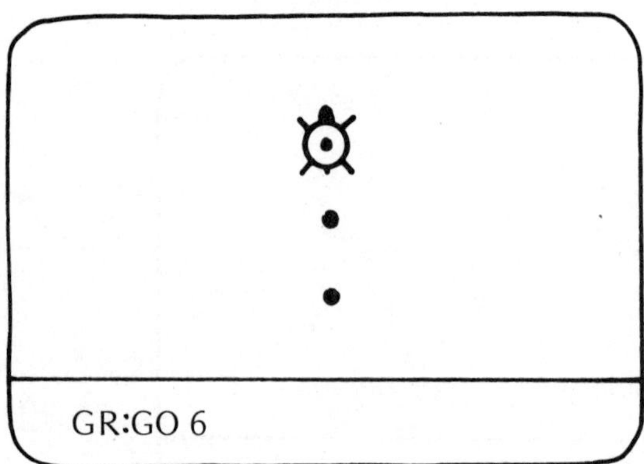

The turtle knows how to back up. Try this:

GR: GO −3

The turtle walks backward 3 steps. Now the screen looks like this (if you imagine the turtle):

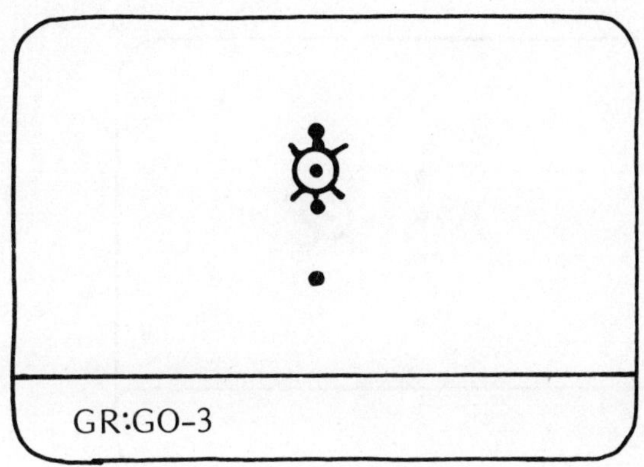

The turtle can do other things beside going forward and backward. This clever turtle knows how to turn any number of degrees to the right or the left. Here's the right-turn instruction for the turtle. Type this:

GR: TURN 90

You won't see any change on your screen because the turtle is invisible. Here is a picture of the turtle who turns 90 degrees to the right:

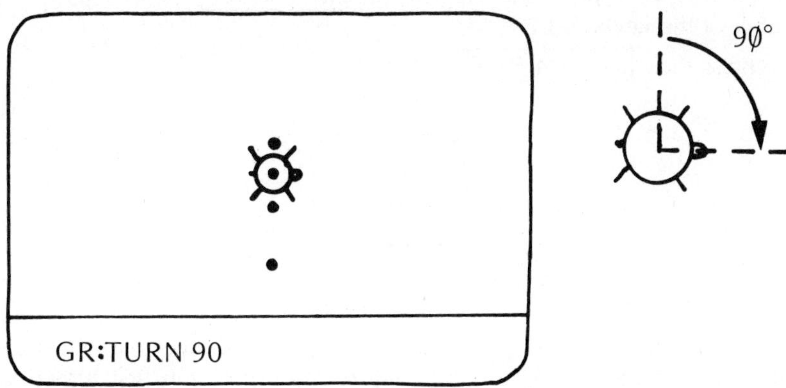

What will happen if you tell the turtle to go ahead now? Type this:

GR: GO 10

Here is what you see on the screen, if you use your imagination:

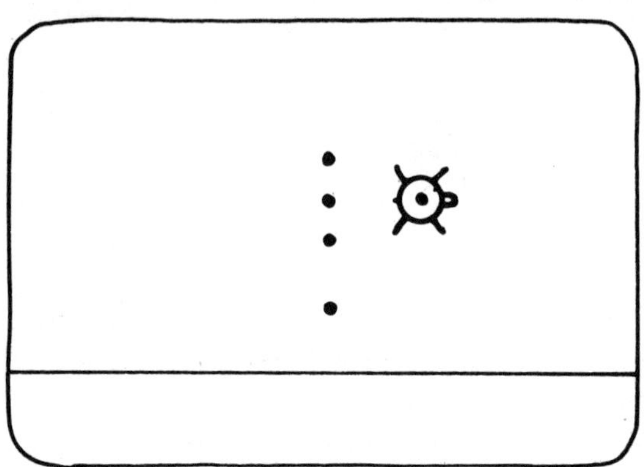

RESETTING THE TURTLE

The turtle has wandered far from the center of the screen. The turtle started from the center of the screen and pointed up toward the top of the screen. How can you get the turtle back to its starting position? The quickest and easiest way is to press the brown $\boxed{\text{SYSTEM RESET}}$ at the upper right corner of the keyboard.

Press the $\boxed{\text{SYSTEM RESET}}$ button.

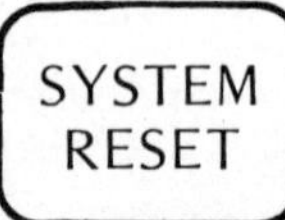

When you press the $\boxed{\text{SYSTEM RESET}}$ button, the screen clears, and the system is reset to almost the way it was when you first turned your computer on. The turtle is back at the middle of the screen, and is pointed up toward the top of the screen. You will learn another method for resetting the turtle a little later.

MANY INSTRUCTIONS PER LINE

You can tell the turtle to do many things all at once. Many commands can be put on the same line. Separate the commands with semicolons. Here is a picture of the semicolon key:

Guess what this line does; press [SYSTEM RESET] and type it.

GR: GO 20; TURN 90; GO 20; TURN 90; GO 20; TURN 90; GO 20

Here is a picture of what you get:

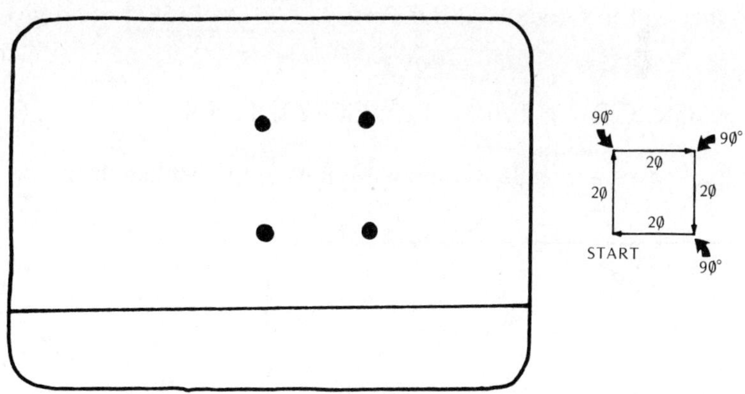

Guess what this line will do; press [SYSTEM RESET] and type it and see.

GR: GO 20; TURN 120; GO 20; TURN 120; GO 20; TURN 120

Here is a picture of the result:

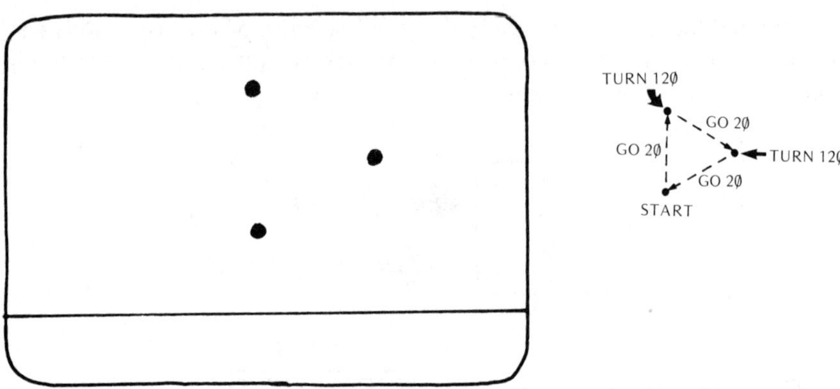

If you want the turtle to turn left instead of right, just put a "-" in front of the turn number. Here is the command to turn left by 120 degrees:

GR: TURN -120

What will this command do? Press SYSTEM RESET   and give it a try.

GR: GO 20; TURN -120; GO 20; TURN -120; GO 20

This line makes a triangle, but now it points to the left like this:

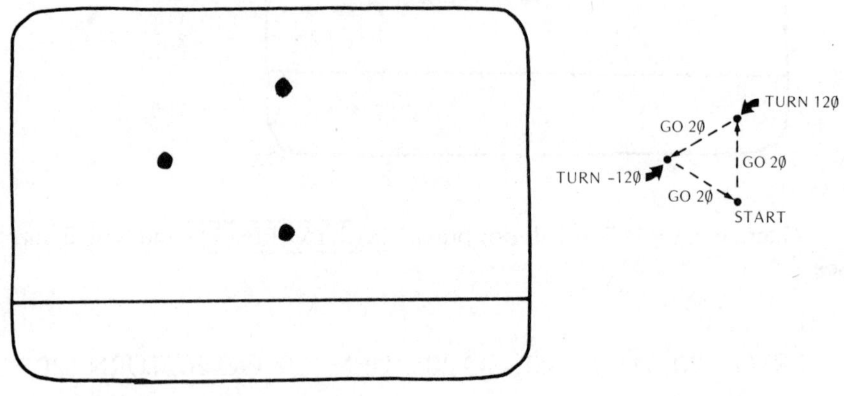

Here is a picture of the turtle with directions written on its back:

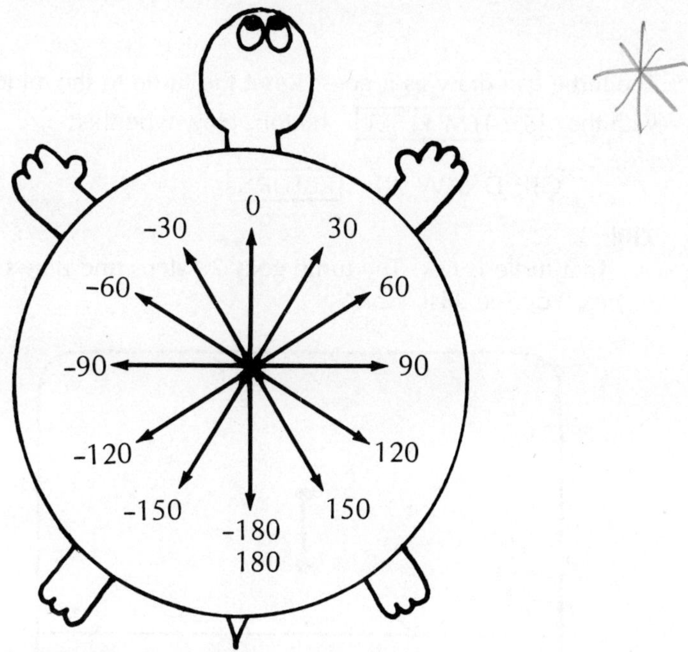

Reset the turtle using the [SYSTEM RESET] button. Now, figure out what this line will do:

GR: TURN -30; GO 10; TURN 60; GO 10; TURN -60; GO 10;
TURN 60; GO 10

Here is a picture:

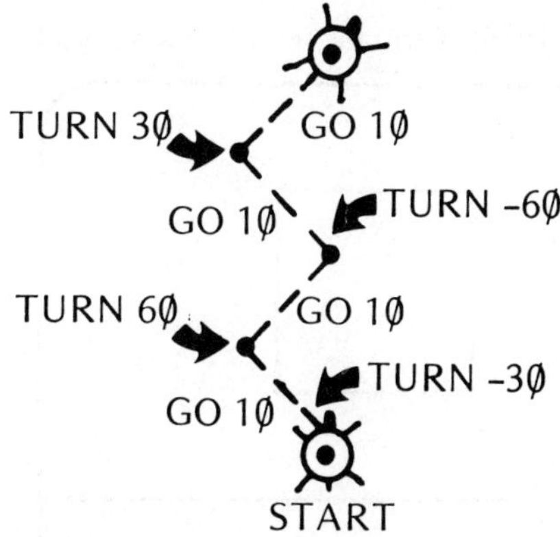

DRAWING

The turtle can draw as it goes. Reset the turtle to the middle of the screen with the $\boxed{\text{SYSTEM RESET}}$ button. Now type this:

GR: DRAW 20 $\boxed{\text{RETURN}}$

ZIP!

That turtle is fast. The turtle goes 20 steps and draws a yellow line as it goes. You see this:

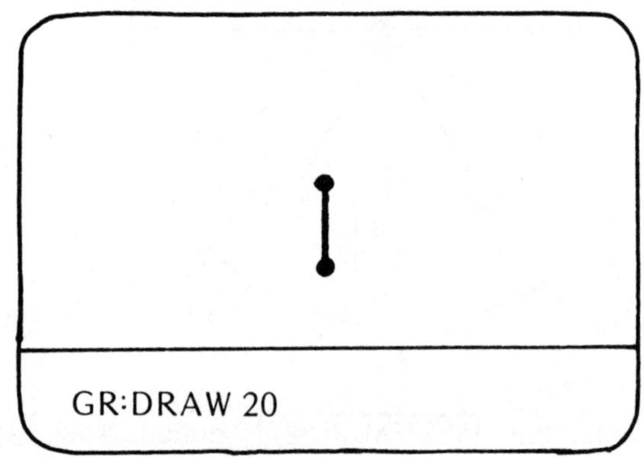

Later you will learn how to draw in other colors.

Press the $\boxed{\text{SYSTEM RESET}}$ button. Type this:

GR: DRAW 20; TURN 90; DRAW 20; TURN 90; DRAW 20; TURN 90; DRAW 20

This instruction draws a square. Here is what you see:

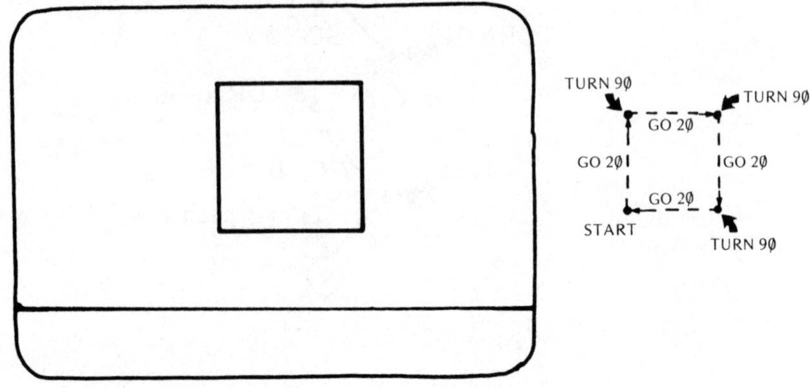

Which direction is the turtle pointed in after the previous instruction?

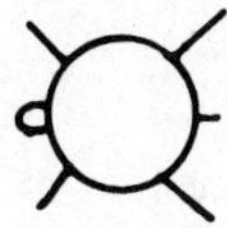

Command the turtle to draw a triangle. Here's a picture of the triangle:

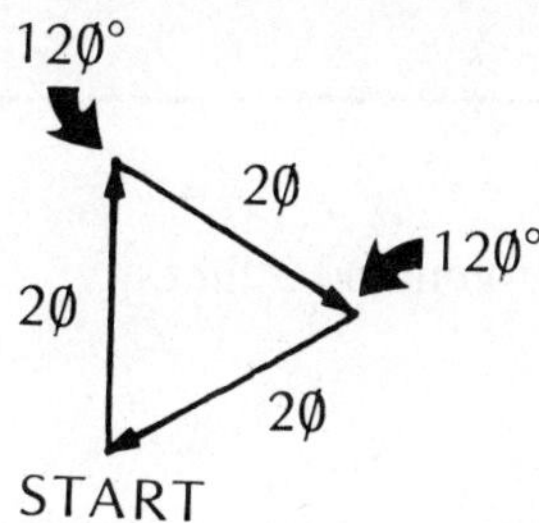

ANSWER:

GR: DRAW 20; TURN 120; DRAW 20; TURN 120; DRAW 20

REPEATING GRAPHICS COMMANDS

Sometimes you will want to repeat some graphics command. The next example shows how to tell the turtle to repeat a command by putting a number in front of the command.

Type this:

GR: 3(GO 6)

You see this:

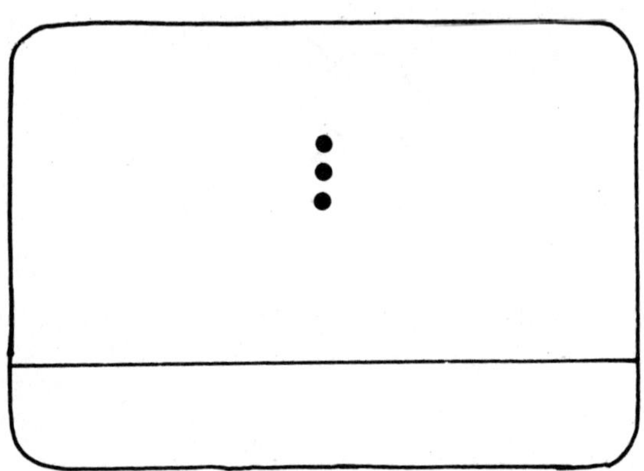

The turtle does the command 3 times.

GR: 3 (GO 6)

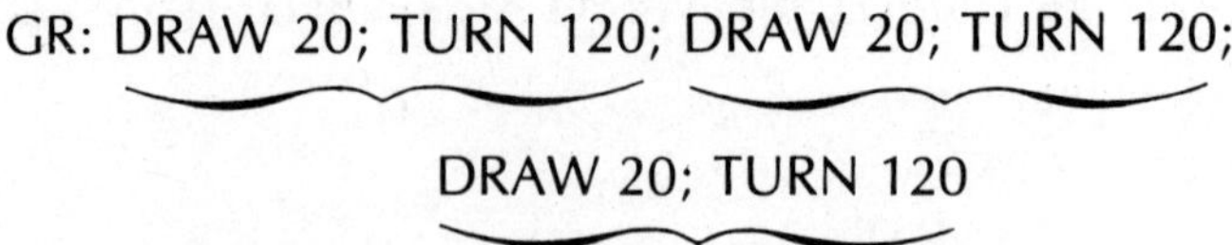

Try this one:

GR: 10(GO 3)

Notice the repetition in this command to draw a triangle:

GR: DRAW 20; TURN 120; DRAW 20; TURN 120;

DRAW 20; TURN 120

You can give a much shorter command now. Try this:

GR: 3(DRAW 20; TURN 120)

The computer repeats the instruction DRAW 20; TURN 120 three times to get a triangle.
What will this command do?

GR: 4(DRAW 20; TURN 90)

ANSWER:

This command will draw a square.

Here is a command that draws a five-sided figure called a pentagon:

GR: 5(DRAW 20; TURN 72)

Give a graphics command to draw a six-sided figure called a hexagon. Here is its picture:

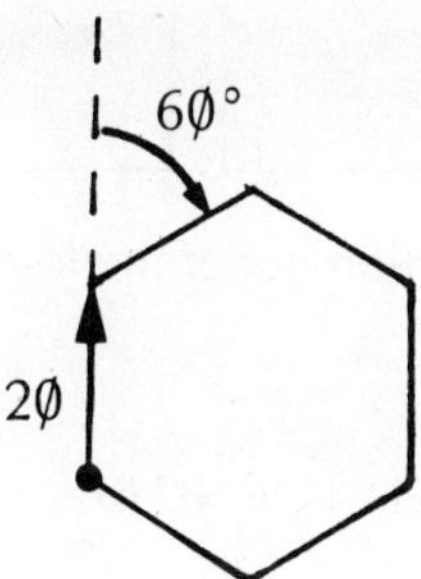

ANSWER:

GR: 6(DRAW 20; TURN 60)

CLEARING THE SCREEN

You can clear the graphics screen without disturbing the turtle's position. The command to do so holds some surprises.
Type this:

GR: CLEAR

The screen is immediately cleared. But our invisible friend the turtle is still at the same position it was before you cleared the screen.

You can make points appear to move by using the CLEAR command. Press SYSTEM RESET   and try this one:

GR: 100(DRAW 4; TURN 18; CLEAR)

The turtle draws a bit, then turns a bit, then clears. The process is repeated and the next bit drawn is in a slightly different position. To your eye the point appears to move in a circle. Here is a picture of the first few screens:

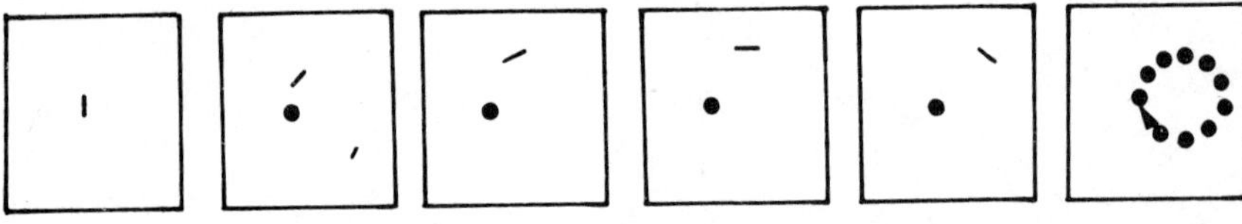

Take the CLEAR instruction out of the last example so that it looks like this:

GR: 100(DRAW 4; TURN 18)

Now the pieces of line run together and you lose the sense of motion.

THE UNKNOWN NUMBER ?

The computer can pick numbers for you. The question mark ? stands for some number. The computer will choose the number. You can't tell what number ? will be. Here is a graphics instruction that uses a number chosen by ?.
Type this:

GR: 100(DRAW 4; TURN ?; CLEAR)

The turtle draws a short line, then turns some angle that it picks, then clears the screen. The process is repeated and the short line appears to move randomly around the screen. The result is a wiggly bug scampering around the screen.

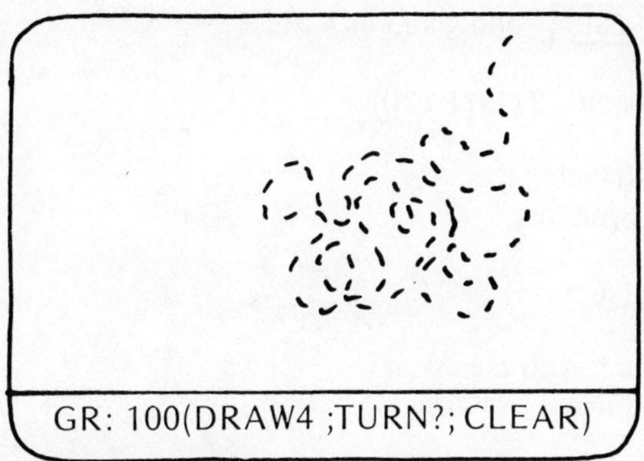

Take the CLEAR command out of the last instruction so that it looks like this:

GR: 100(DRAW 4; TURN ?)

Now you can see the bug's path as it moves.

PEN COLORS

You can tell the turtle to change pens. What color would you like? The colors available are YELLOW, RED, and BLUE. The pen is YELLOW unless you change it.

Type this:

GR: PEN RED

Now the turtle's pen is red. The pen will stay red until you change it or turn off the computer. You can check that the pen color is red by drawing something.

Here is something simple to draw. Press SYSTEM RESET and type this:

GR: DRAW 30

Ahh. A lovely red line.

Press SYSTEM RESET and give this a try:

GR: 3(DRAW 30; TURN 120)

You see a lovely red triangle.
Try a BLUE pen. Type this:

GR: PEN BLUE

Now the pen is blue until you change it.
Here is a six-sided figure, a hexagon:

GR: 6(DRAW 20; TURN 60)

You see a blue hexagon. You can put more sides on the figure and it will look like a circle. Press SYSTEM RESET and type this:

GR: 60(DRAW 2; TURN 6)

You see this:

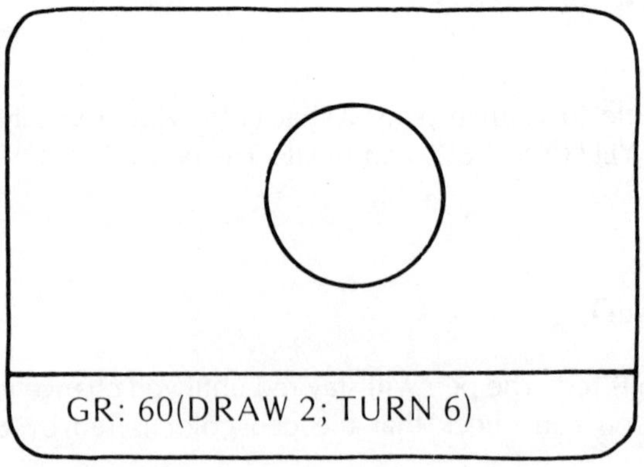

You can change pens in the middle of a drawing. Here is a three-colored dotted line. Press SYSTEM RESET and type this:

GR: 6(PEN RED; DRAW 4; PEN BLUE; DRAW 4; PEN
YELLOW; DRAW 4)

PEN UP

The turtle has two more pens to use.

You can tell the turtle to pick up the pen. When the pen is up, the turtle leaves no tracks.

Press SYSTEM RESET   and type this:

GR: PEN UP: DRAW 30

What do you expect to see? Not much. An invisible turtle with its pen up doesn't leave any clues. The turtle's pen stays up until you give the pen a color.

Press SYSTEM RESET   and try this:

GR: 3(PEN RED; DRAW 6; PEN UP; DRAW 6)

You see a dashed line like this:

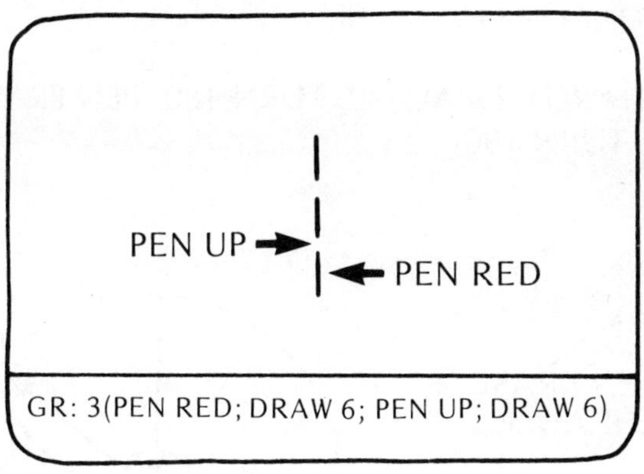

Remember the number ?? The computer will get a number for you when it sees the question mark. Let's let the computer do some work. Press SYSTEM RESET   and try this:

GR: 100(PEN YELLOW; DRAW 4; PEN UP; TURN ?; DRAW 4)

PEN ERASE

The turtle has an eraser to use. The eraser really writes in the color BLACK. Black is the color of the background. If you draw with the eraser, you write in the background color. Anywhere the turtle draws gets blacked out.
   Press [SYSTEM RESET]   and try this:

   GR: PEN ERASE; DRAW 20

You don't see anything happen. The turtle draws in black on a black screen. That's hard to see.
   Press [SYSTEM RESET]   and try this:

   GR: PEN YELLOW; DRAW 30; PEN ERASE; DRAW -30

Look quick. The computer will draw and erase fast.
   Here is an instruction that makes a clock hand rotate. The turtle draws out from the center in red, then the turtle erases as it draws back to the center. Next, the turtle turns a bit and repeats the process. Press [SYSTEM RESET] and give it a try.

   GR: 360(PEN RED; DRAW 30; TURN 180; PEN ERASE;
   DRAW 30; TURN 190)

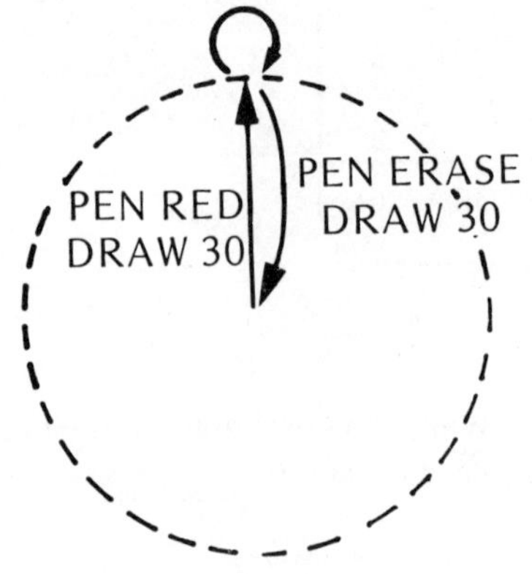

SELF-TEST ON CHAPTER 4

1. What will this command do?

    GR: DRAW 5; GO 5; DRAW 5

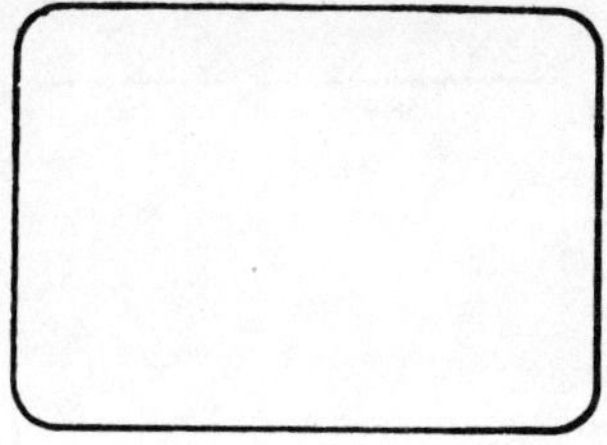

2. What will this command do?

    GR: PEN RED; TURN 90; GO 10

3. What will this command do?

    GR: 3(DRAW 10; TURN 120)

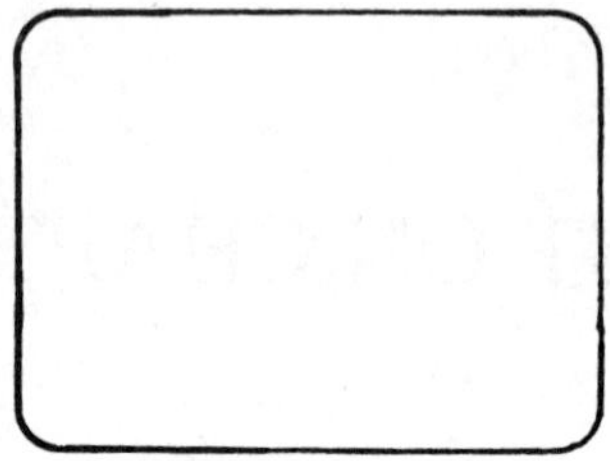

4. What will this command do?

GR: 5(DRAW 10; TURN ?)

5. Write a command to draw a red square with sides 10 steps long.

____

____

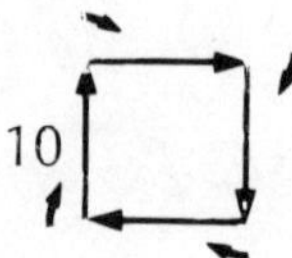

6. What command tells the turtle to draw for 10 steps while moving backwards?

7. What will this command do?

GR: 100(DRAW 4; TURN ?; CLEAR)

8. In what direction is the turtle pointed after you press
   SYSTEM RESET ?

   ____

9. Write a command to make a figure that looks like this:

   ____

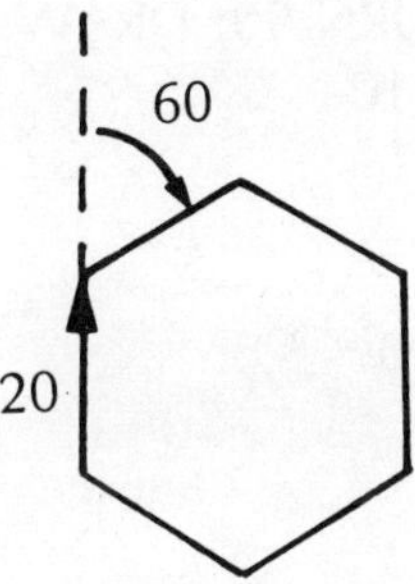

10. Write a command to make a figure like this:

   ____

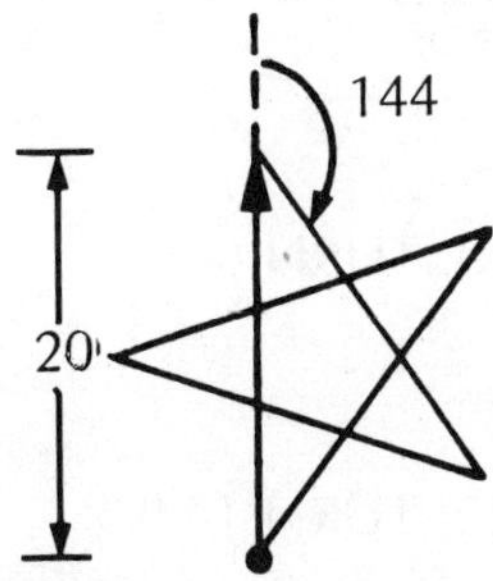

ANSWERS:

1.   2.   3.   4.

5.

GR: 4(DRAW 10; TURN 90)

You could also do it this way:

GR: DRAW 10: TURN 90; DRAW 10; TURN 90; DRAW 10; TURN 90; DRAW 10

6.

GR: DRAW -10

7. The command

GR: 100(DRAW 4; TURN ?; CLEAR)

will repeat the commands inside the parentheses 100 times. The turtle will draw a short line, turn a random angle, then clear the screen and repeat the process. The result will be a wiggly, moving blip.

8. When SYSTEM RESET is pressed, the turtle goes to the middle of the screen and points up.

9.

GR: 6(DRAW 20; TURN 60)

10.

GR: 5(DRAW 20; TURN 144)

SUMMARY OF CHAPTER 4

In this chapter you learned:

- that your computer has an invisible graphics turtle
- how to give commands to the graphics turtle to make it draw
- that GR: alerts the graphics turtle for your commands
- that the graphics turtle can be told to GO some number of steps
- that the turtle can be told to TURN some number of degrees
- that the turtle can be told to DRAW for some number of steps
- that the ⬚SYSTEM RESET⬚ button clears the screen and sends the turtle to the center of the screen, pointing up
- that many instructions, separated by semicolons, can be given on one line
- how to quickly draw triangles, squares, and other figures
- that a command can be repeated by putting a number in front
- that the command CLEAR clears the graphic screen
- how to make your drawings appear to move
- that the computer replaces the question mark ? with a number
- that the turtle has three pen colors: YELLOW, RED, and BLUE
- that YELLOW is the pen color unless you set another
- that the command PEN UP lifts the turtle's pen so it won't draw
- that the command PEN ERASE turns the pen into an eraser

USING PROGRAM MODULES

5

The PILOT language is designed to help you think clearly. PILOT makes it easy to break big tasks into small tasks called modules. In this chapter you will learn:

- how to build big programs out of small programs called modules
- how to make and store your own library of program modules
- how to use modules that are stored in memory
- how to use simple modules to draw complex figures
- how to write programs in a style that makes them easy to read

PROGRAM MODULES

A module is a chunk. A module is a particular bunch of things.

Houses that are put together in big chunks are called modular houses. A modular house is built out of house modules.

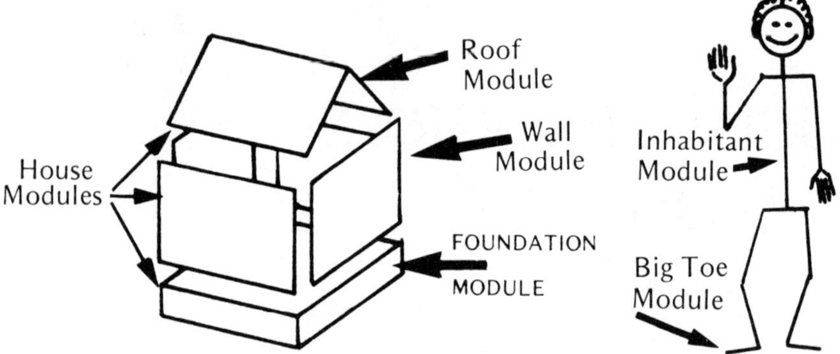

A modular program is a program built out of program modules.

You can plan your day in terms of modules. Let's see now. You get up, then you get ready, then you go. Each of these activities is a module which consists of many simpler activities. The simpler activities can also be modules. A module is any chunk that you can think about. A module has a comfortable size. It is big enough to be useful, but small enough to understand.

Here is an example of a PILOT program module. Type NEW to clear out any old programs, and then type this:

```
100 *TRIANGLE         THE MODULE IS CALLED *TRIANGLE
110 GR: 3(DRAW 20; TURN 120)
120 E:          E: MARKS THE END OF THE MODULE
```

The module starts with its name (*TRIANGLE). The module ends with the end command E:.

THE USEFUL USE COMMAND

The program module called *TRIANGLE is stored in the computer's memory. You can call any module by name and use it whenever you want.

Press   SYSTEM RESET , then type this:

U: *TRIANGLE   RETURN

The triangle appears on the screen:

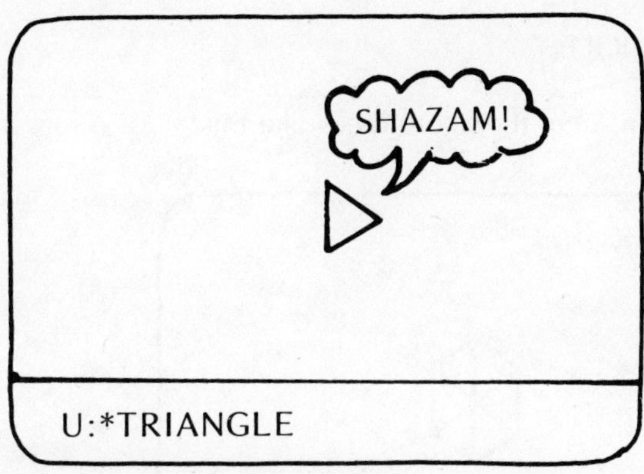

The computer finds the module called *TRIANGLE and follows the instructions to the end. The end of the module is marked by the end command E:.

Let's rotate the turtle a bit before using *TRIANGLE again. Type this:

GR: TURN 60   [RETURN]
U: *TRIANGLE   [RETURN]

You see this:

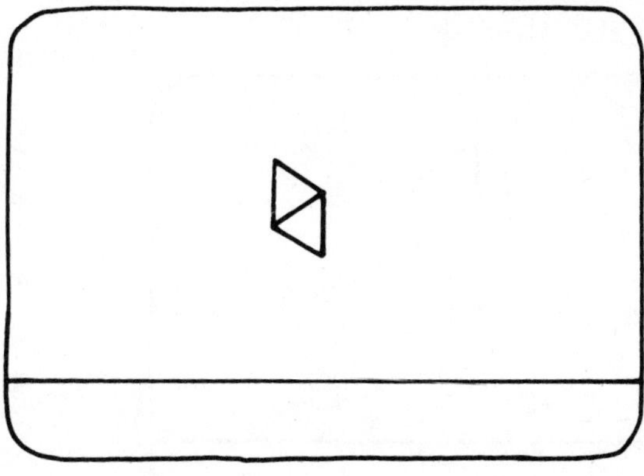

Do it one more time:

> GR: TURN 60
> U: *TRIANGLE

Do it once again, until the figure looks like this:

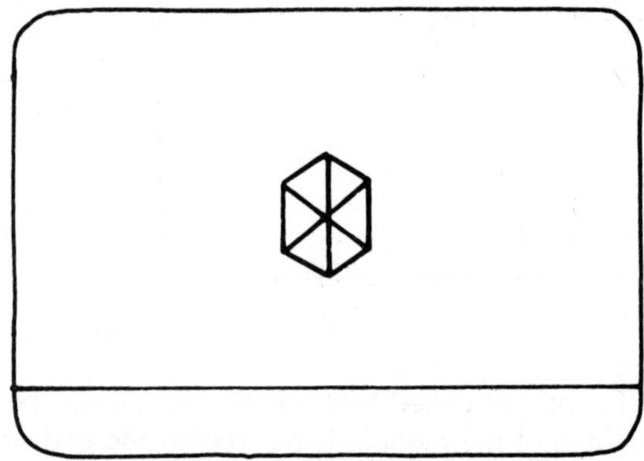

Isn't that lovely? You can send the turtle anyplace on the screen and have it draw a triangle there.

Let's move the turtle to the top of the screen, and then use *TRIANGLE. Press SYSTEM RESET   and type this:

> GR: GO 20
> U: *TRIANGLE

You see this:

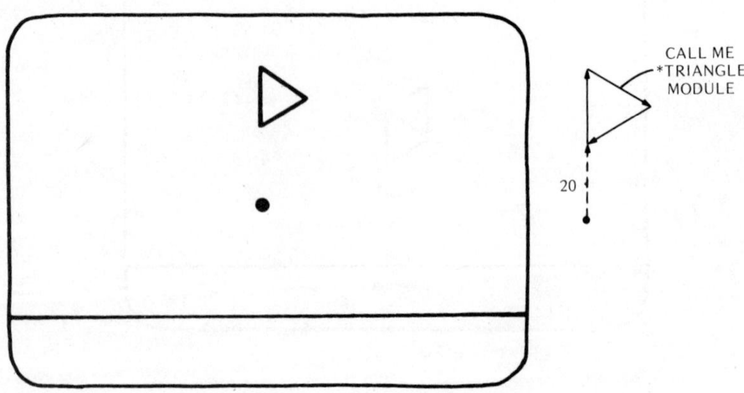

MANY MODULES CAN BE MADE

Many modules can be saved in the computer's memory at the same time. In fact, you can store dozens and dozens of different modules in memory at the same time. Let's add a module that draws a square.

Type this module:

    200 *SQUARE ☞ THIS IS CALLED *SQUARE
    210 GR: 4(DRAW 20; TURN 90)
    220 E: ☞ THE END OF THE MODULE

Now, both of the modules *TRIANGLE and *SQUARE are stored in the computer's memory. Either can be used.

Type this:

    U: *SQUARE

The square appears on the screen.

Now, type this:

    U: *TRIANGLE

The triangle appears inside of the square. You see this on the screen:

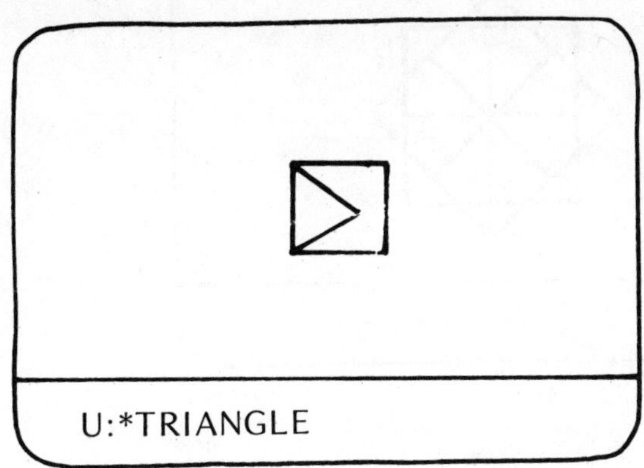

Press SYSTEM RESET and type this:

    GR: TURN 45
    U: *SQUARE

The turtle turned 45 degrees before drawing the square. You see this:

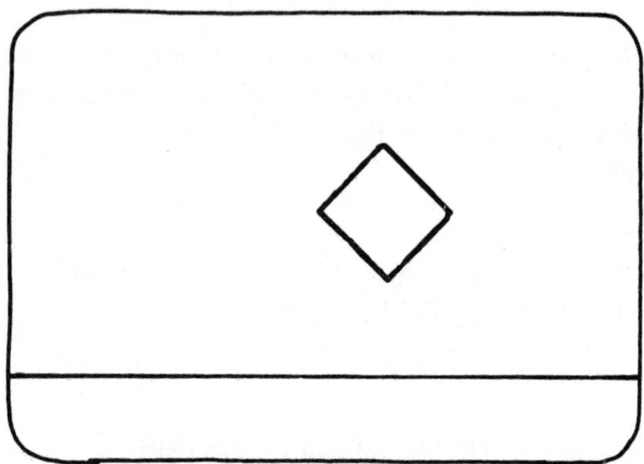

Repeat the previous commands:

```
GR: TURN 45
U: *SQUARE
```

Repeat the commands until the screen looks like this:

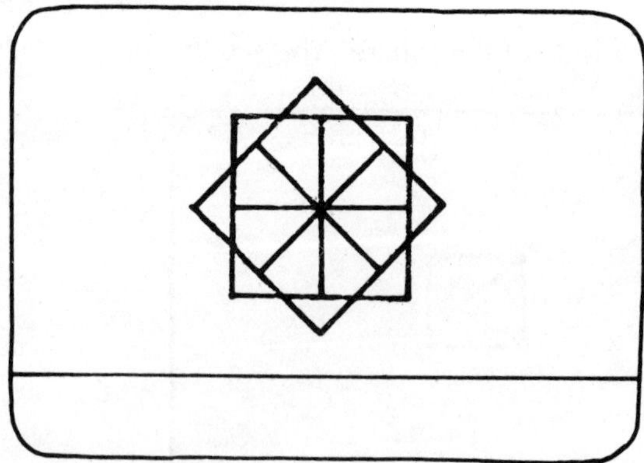

A MODULAR HOUSE

You can use the modules *TRIANGLE and *SQUARE to construct a module called *HOUSE.

The module *HOUSE will draw a house like this:

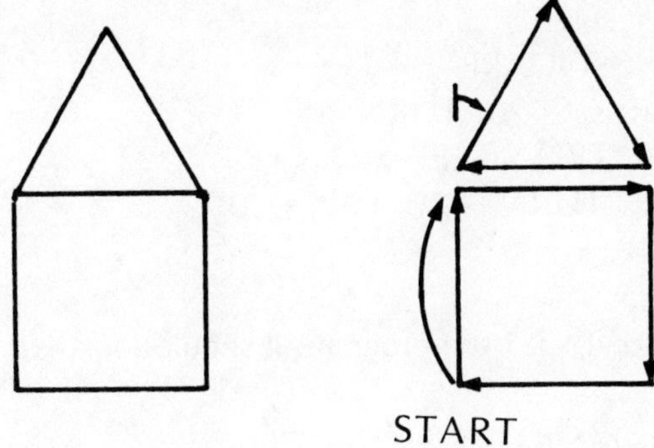

Here is a story board that shows the turtle drawing the house:

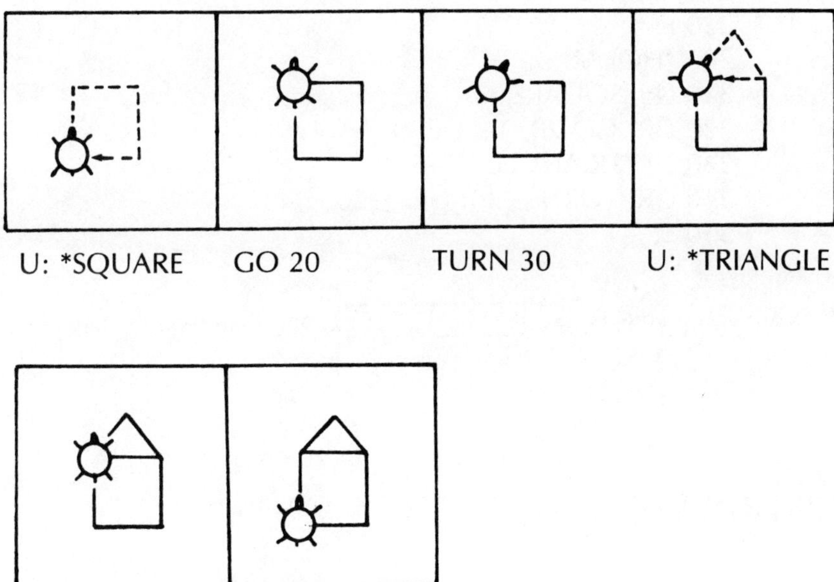

The module *HOUSE will use the modules *TRIANGLE and *SQUARE that are still stored in memory.

Add these lines to the program in the computer's memory:

```
300 *HOUSE
310 U: *SQUARE
320 GR: GO 20; TURN 30
330 U: *TRIANGLE
340 GR: TURN −30; GO −20
350 E:
```

When you are done, LIST the program. It should look like this:

```
100 *TRIANGLE
110 GR: 3(DRAW 20; TURN 120)
120 E:
200 *SQUARE
210 GR: 4(DRAW 20; TURN 90)
220 E:
300 *HOUSE
310 U: *SQUARE
320 GR: GO 20; TURN 30
330 U: *TRIANGLE
340 GR: TURN −30; GO −20
350 E:
```

Are you ready? Press   SYSTEM RESET   and then type this:

```
U: *HOUSE
```

PROGRAMMING STYLE

You probably noticed that long programs begin to look complicated. There are some tricks available in PILOT that will help you make long programs look simple. That's what programming style is all about, making programs easy to read and understand.

Here is the previous program with a few spaces added in to make it easier to read. The commas (,) that you see are just placeholders that allow spaces to be added.

```
100 *TRIANGLE
110 , GR: 3(DRAW 20; TURN 120)
120 , E:
200 *SQUARE
210 , GR: 4(DRAW 20; TURN 90)
220 , E:
300 *HOUSE
310 , U: *SQUARE
320 , GR: GO 20; TURN 30
330 , U: *TRIANGLE
340 , GR: TURN −30; GO −20
350 , E:
```

Now you can see where each module starts and ends. It is much easier to read the program now.

You can easily put your program into a stylish form. First, LIST your program so that it appears on the screen. Here is what the first two lines of your program look like:

```
100 *TRIANGLE
120 GR: 3(DRAW 20; TURN 120)
```

Now, use the control arrows to move the cursor over the first G in line 120, like this:

```
120  [G] R: 3(DRAW 20; TURN 120)
```

Hold the [CTRL] key down and type the [INSERT] key three times. You see this:

```
120  [ ]  GR: 3(DRAW 20; TURN 120)
```

The letters scoot to the right, and spaces are inserted.

Now, type a comma, like this:

```
120 , GR: 3(DRAW 20; TURN 120)
```

Press ⎡RETURN⎤ and this new stylish line is inserted in your list of stored commands. To see that the change worked, type

LIST

The comma is needed. If you don't put in the comma, the computer tidies up your lines for you, and takes out all unnecessary spaces, even the ones you want. The comma stops the computer from taking out your spaces.

Start now to do stylish programming.

But keep the modules in your computer a while longer. There are still a few things to do.

JUMPING

There will be many times when you will want your program to run over and over again. The JUMP command J: is just what you need.

Add this program to your growing program list:

```
400 *ROCKET
410 , U: *HOUSE
420 , GR: TURN 10; GO 5; CLEAR
430 , J: *ROCKET          JUMP TO *ROCKET
```

The command J: *ROCKET tells the computer to start at the line labeled *ROCKET and continue from there.

Type this:

U: *ROCKET   ⎡RETURN⎤

You see the house fly around in a big circle:

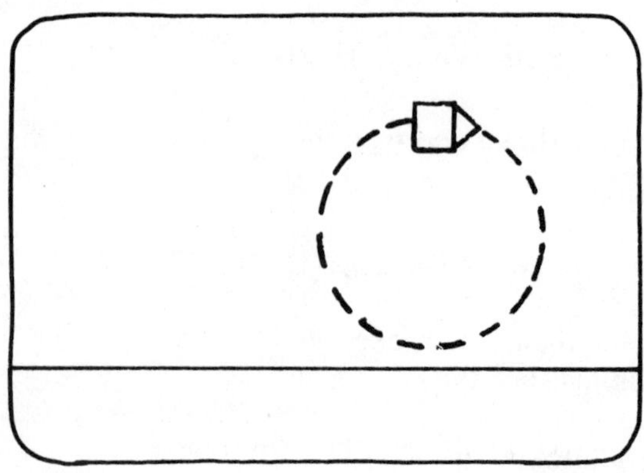

Press the BREAK key to stop the program.

LIST the program. Use the control arrows to move the cursor to the semicolon (;) just before the word CLEAR in line 420.

420 , GR: TURN 10; GO 5 ; CLEAR

Now, type the CTRL   DELETE key to remove '; CLEAR'.
Press RETURN to enter the new line into program memory. RUN the program. What does it do now that the CLEAR command is gone?

You see a circular path composed of rockets. Press the BREAK key to stop the program.

Let's let the computer choose the turn number in line 420. Change line 420 to this:

420 , GR: TURN ?; GO 4

Now, use *ROCKET. Type this:

U: *ROCKET

What happens?

You see a wandering path of houses. Press the BREAK key to stop the program.

A MYSTERY COMMAND

Here is another change to line 420. Type this:

420 , GR: TURN ?\20; GO 10; CLEAR

You'll learn about ?\20 later. Try the program. Type

U: *ROCKET

You see a rocket ship wobble around in circles on the screen.

Say goodbye to *ROCKET, *HOUSE, *TRIANGLE, and *SQUARE. It is time to move on. If you want to save these, or any other programs that you write, then you should read Appendix A at the back of the book. It will tell you how to save programs on your cassette recorder or floppy disk. You won't need to save anything to read the rest of this book.

Type this to clear the old programs out of program memory:

NEW   RETURN

Onward and upward.

MORE JUMPING

Here is a short program that draws a square. This program is slightly different from the one you used before. Type this:

```
10 *TOP
20 , GR: DRAW 10
30 , GR: TURN 90
40 , J: *TOP
RUN
```

When you run this program, you see a small square. The program keeps drawing the square over and over. There are many ways to accomplish the same task. Your programs might look different than ours, yet still be correct.

If your program works, then it is right. Press the BREAK key to stop the program.

A minor change will make the last program a lot more exciting. Try this change to line 30:

```
30 GR: TURN ?
RUN
```

You see something like this:

The bug wiggles around the screen leaving a trail.

SOME MYSTERY COMMANDS

Do you like mysteries? Here are some commands that tell the the computer to make up numbers in special ways. You'll learn more about these commands later.

Change line 30 to this:

```
30 GR: TURN ?\90
RUN
```

The bug still moves at random, but it seems good at going in rough circles. You see something like this:

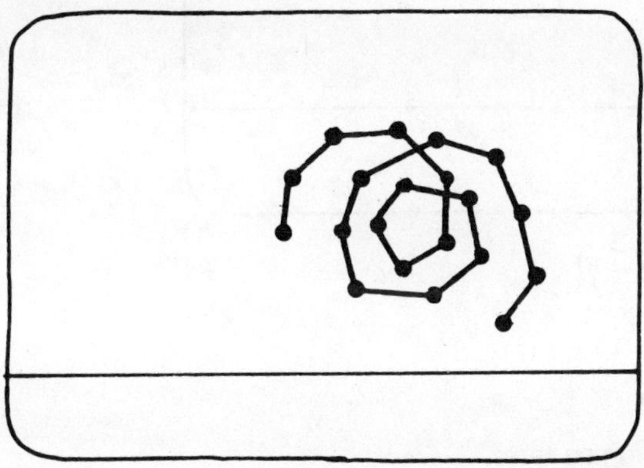

Try this new version of line 30. It works quite differently than the last programs.

```
30 GR: TURN ?\4*90
RUN
```

You see something like this:

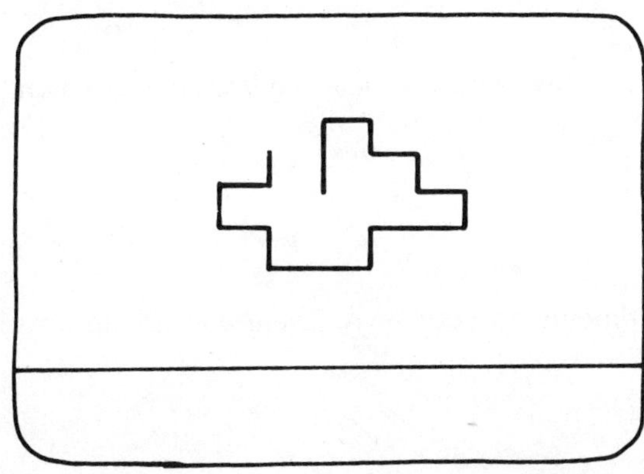

Now for a change in line 20. Do this:

    20 GR: DRAW ?\5
    RUN

This changes things a lot. Now the screen looks like this:

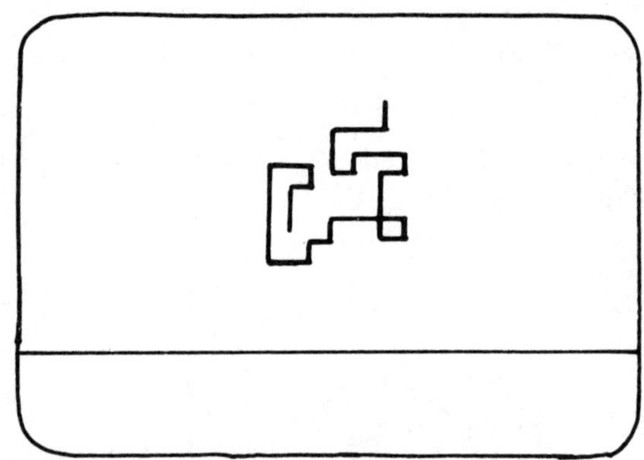

Let's add some sound:

    15 SO: 1
    35 SO:

LIST the program. You see this:

    10 *TOP
    15 SO: 1
    20 GR: DRAW ?\5
    30 GR: TURN ?\4*90
    35 SO:
    40 J: *TOP

Now, RUN the program. Now you can hear the lines being drawn.
    Add a pause:

    25 PA: 10
    RUN

Now, try a few experiments on your own. There are infinite possibilities
here.

SELF-TEST ON CHAPTER 5

1. What is on the first line of a PILOT module? _______
2. What is at the beginning of every module name? _______
3. What does this module do?

        10 * THIS
        20 GR: PEN RED; DRAW 5
        30 E:

4. What does a leading comma do in a program line?

   ____

5. How would you stop this program?

        10 *TOP
        20 J:TOP

   ____

6. Write a program module called *DOT that will draw a single red dot
   when it is used.

        10 _______________________________________
        20 _______________________________________
        30 _______________________________________

7. Here's a program module that doesn't seem to work properly. Fix it so
   that it will work as a module should.

        10 *THAT
        20 GR: DRAW 5

   ____

8. The module *TRIANGLE makes a triangle with side 20 when it is used. Tell what this next module will do when it is used:

```
500 *THESE
510 , U: *TRIANGLE
520 , GR: TURN 180
530 , U: *TRIANGLE
540 , E:
```

9. What will this program do when run?

```
10 *TOP
20 , GR: DRAW 5; TURN 10; CLEAR
30 , J:*TOP
```

10. Suppose that *SQUARE is stored in program memory. Write a program module that will draw four squares like this:

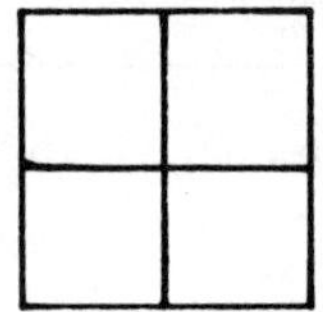

```
 10 ____________________________________
 20 ____________________________________
 30 ____________________________________
 40 ____________________________________
 50 ____________________________________
 60 ____________________________________
 70 ____________________________________
 80 ____________________________________
 90 ____________________________________
100 ____________________________________
```

ANSWERS:

1. The first line of a PILOT module is the name of the module.
2. The name of a module is always preceded by an asterisk (*).

3. The module *THIS draws a short red line at the position, and in the direction, of the turtle.

4. A leading comma in a program line is used as a placeholder. It tells the computer to leave in the spaces that follow.

5. The   BREAK   key is used to stop programs while they are running. The   SYSTEM RESET   button will also work, but   BREAK   is preferred.

6. Here is one example of a program that draws a single red dot:

```
10 *DOT
20 GR: PEN RED; GO 0
30 E:
```

7. The program module needs an end command

```
30 E:
```

8. The module *THESE will draw a figure at the position, and oriented in the direction, of the turtle. The figure looks like this:

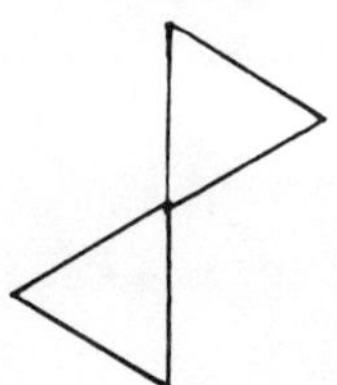

9. The program will repeatedly draw, clear the screen, and move. The result will be a short line that appears to move in a circle.

10.

```
10 *FOUR
20 , U: *SQUARE
30 , GR: TURN 90
40 , U: *SQUARE
50 , GR: TURN 90
60 , U: *SQUARE
70 , GR: TURN 90
80 , U: *SQUARE
90 , GR: TURN 90
100 , E:
```

SUMMARY OF CHAPTER 5

In this chapter you learned:

- that PILOT programs can be built up from simple program modules
- that a program module starts with its name
- that a module name starts with an asterisk *
- that the USE command U: calls modules into action
- that the end command E: marks the end of a module
- that modules may be used by other program modules
- that a comma is used to indent lines for purposes of style
- that the JUMP command J: tells the computer to jump to a named line
- that there may be many ways to do the same programming job

6
READING AND WRITING

This chapter is about reading and writing, and about accepting and matching. Your computer will accept whatever you type. The computer will store it away. The computer can check what is typed to see if it matches special words and letters that you choose. In this chapter you will learn:

- how to make the typer tell things on the screen
- how to make the computer stop and pay attention to what you type
- how to make stories that go just as fast as the reader wants
- how to give names to names and other messages
- how to store messages in the computer and get them back
- how to write a thank-you letter that works for every occasion
- how to make the computer type the proper thing at the proper time
- how to make the computer ask questions and check answers
- how to make the matcher look for a word hidden in an answer

THE TYPER TELLS

The typer types letters on the screen. The command T: calls the typer to work.

Here is a line that commands the typer to tell something. Give it a try:

T: T IS FOR TELL

When you press   RETURN   , you see this:

T IS FOR TELL

Remember the pause command? This next example uses the pause command PA: 600 to make the computer pause 10 seconds before it calls the typer into action. Type NEW and give this a try:

```
10 PA: 600        PAUSE FOR 600 JIFFIES (10 SECONDS)
20 T: HELP, HELP
30 PA: 180
40 T: I'M TRAPPED IN THE COMPUTER
50 PA: 120
60 T: GET ME OUT
RUN
```

When you RUN this program, nothing happens for 600 jiffies. (That's 10 seconds.) Then the computer types

HELP, HELP

The computer pauses again. It waits 180 jiffies. (That's 3 seconds.) Then the computer types

I'M TRAPPED IN THE COMPUTER

Then it waits 120 jiffies (2 seconds) and types

GET ME OUT

TEASE

Here is a program that will trap your friends. They won't be able to get away. The name of the program is *TEASE. You can see why.

Type NEW and give this a try:

```
100 *TEASE
110 SO: 31        SOUND ON
120 PA: 360       PAUSE 6 SECONDS
130 T: MAY I HAVE YOUR ATTENTION PLEASE
140 PA: 360       PAUSE 6 SECONDS
150 T: (ESC)(SHIFT)(CLEAR)       THIS CLEARS THE
                                         SCREEN
160 PA: 180       PAUSE 3 SECONDS
170 SO:           SOUND OFF
180 T: ONE MOMENT PLEASE
190 PA: 3600      PAUSE FOR 1 MINUTE
```

If this program doesn't drive your friends crazy, then add a few more lines. How long can you keep someone waiting for the computer to do something?

Here is some space for you to add a few lines of your own:

```
200 ______________________________________________
210 ______________________________________________
220 ______________________________________________
230 ______________________________________________
240 ______________________________________________
250 ______________________________________________
```

Go on as long as you like. Get someone to try your program.

GETTING THE COMPUTER TO LISTEN

So far you have made the computer do all the talking, or at least all the telling, or at least all the typing. You can make the computer pay attention to what you type. The answering service pays attention and accepts messages. The command A: calls the answering service into action. The answering service accepts what you type. It listens until you press the RETURN key. Then it knows you are finished.

Type this short program:

```
10 T: PRESS THE (RETURN) KEY TO GO ON
20 A:
30 T: PRESS IT AGAIN
40 A:
50 T: THAT'S ALL
RUN
```

When you RUN this program, the computer types

PRESS THE (RETURN) KEY TO GO ON

Then the computer stops. The answering service listens for your message. As soon as you press [RETURN] , the computer goes on to the next line and types

PRESS IT AGAIN

Then the computer stops again and listens for your message. When you press [RETURN] , the computer goes on to the next line and types:

THAT'S ALL

Write a program that counts to 3 as you press the [RETURN] key. Here is what should happen:

```
PRESS (RETURN) 👉 THE COMPUTER SAYS THIS
[RETURN] 👉 YOU PRESS [RETURN]
1 👉 THE COMPUTER TYPES THIS
[RETURN] 👉 YOU PRESS [RETURN]
2 👉 THE COMPUTER TYPES THIS
[RETURN] 👉 YOU PRESS [RETURN]
3 👉 THE COMPUTER TYPES THIS
```

Here is some space for your program:

```
10 T: PRESS [RETURN]
20 _______________________________________
```

```
30 _______________________________________________
40 _______________________________________________
50 _______________________________________________
60 _______________________________________________
70 _______________________________________________
```

Add some sound to your program. When the number 1 appears, play sound 1. When the number 2 appears, play sound 2. When the number 3 appears, play sound 3.

ANSWER: Here is one possible program to type the numbers and play the sounds:

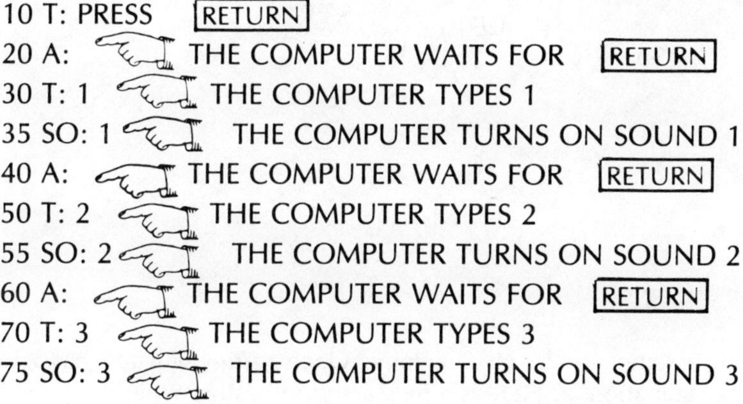

A STORY TELLER

You can use the A: command to write computer stories that go just as fast as the reader wants the story to go. Type NEW and try this:

```
10 T: YOU ARE WALKING ALONG A PATH IN A DENSE
FOREST
20 A:
30 T: YOU SEE A PATCH OF LIGHT AHEAD OF YOU
40 A:
50 T: YOU ENTER A CLEARING
60 A:
```

Now it's your turn. What do you suppose you see in the clearing? What next, and what after that? Be creative. It's your story.

    70 ____
    80 ____
    90 ____

Take as much space and time as you need.

MESSAGE NAMES

A message is just a bunch of letters strung together.

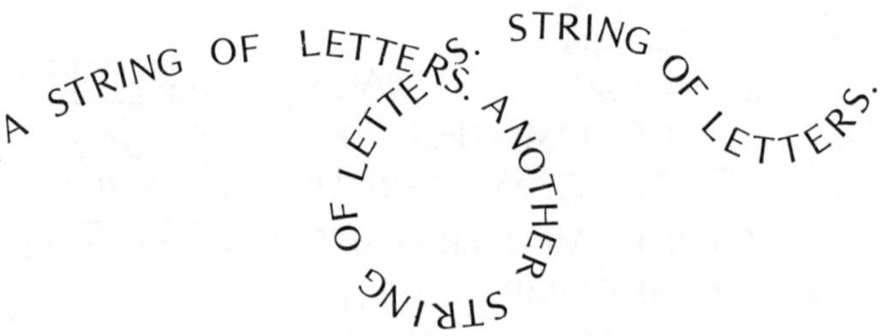

A string of letters can be given a name. Once a string of letters has a name, you can talk about it. Here is a message string called $MESS:

JO, CALL FLO ABOUT MO

Now you can talk about $MESS.

A SHORT AND PAINLESS QUIZ:

Mark each of these true or false:

$MESS has a comma in it. T/F
$MESS contains the word OUT someplace in it. T/F
$MESS contains 22 letters. T/F

ANSWERS: T, T, F.

STORING MESSAGES BY NAME

You can tell the answering service to store messages for you. Here is how you tell the answering service to store the message $MESS. Type this:

A: $MESS = JO, CALL FLO ABOUT MO   RETURN

The answering service accepts the message, names it $MESS, and stores it safely away in the computer memory.

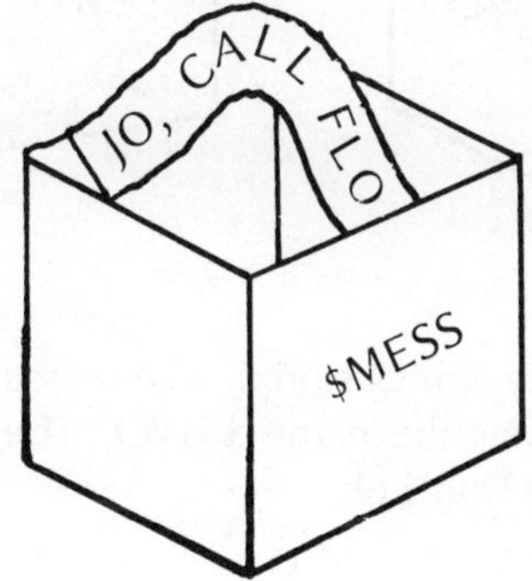

You can get the message string back anytime you wish. Type this:

T: $MESS

You see this:

JO, CALL FLO ABOUT MO

The typer gets the message named $MESS and types it out for you. The message string is still stored. You can use it again whenever you want.

$ MEANS STRING

That $ sign in the name $MESS is no accident. Names of message strings always start with $. The $ tells the computer that a string name is coming. You can think of $ as standing for the S in String.

You can store lots of message strings.

Type this:

A: $ONE = THIS   RETURN
A: $TWO = IS   RETURN

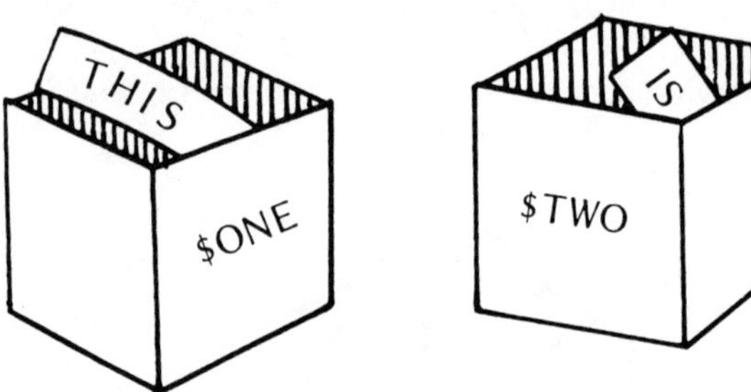

Now you've got two more strings stored. The message THIS has the name $ONE. The message IS has the name $TWO. The name happens to be longer than the message. That's ok.

Type this:

T: $ONE $TWO

The typer finds $ONE and types the message THIS, then puts in a space, then finds $TWO and types IS. You see this:

THIS IS

What will this command print?

T: $TWO $ONE

____

What will this command print?

T: $ONE $TWO $ONE

____

ANSWERS: IS THIS; THIS IS THIS.

You can use words mixed with message strings. Try this:

    T: JO $TWO TALL

You see this:

    JO IS TALL

THANK-YOU LETTER

Have you written your thank-you letters for Christmas? Should you send some letters to your friends? Here is a program that will be very helpful. Type this program:

    110 T: DEAR $NAME
    120 T: THANKS FOR THE $GIFT. I APPRECIATE IT A LOT.
    130 T: YOURS,
    140 T: NORDLEBERT

Now, before you run this program, you should tell the computer what the message strings $NAME and $GIFT stand for. Here's an example:

    A: $NAME = UNCLE CLEM,   [RETURN]
    A: $GIFT = CLAM LEASH   [RETURN]

Now type RUN, and you see this:

    DEAR UNCLE CLEM,
    THANKS FOR THE CLAM LEASH. I APPRECIATE IT A LOT.
    YOURS,
    NORDLEBERT

If Aunt Kate sent you a nifty pair of purple earmuffs, you would change the message strings like this:

    A:$NAME = AUNT KATE
    A:$GIFT = NIFTY PURPLE EARMUFFS

Now when you RUN the program, you see:

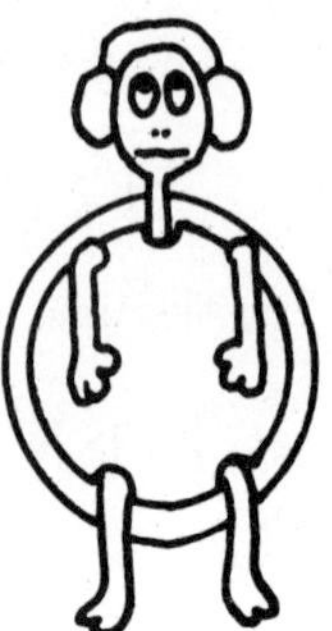

```
DEAR AUNT KATE,
THANKS FOR THE NIFTY PURPLE EARMUFFS. I
APPRECIATE IT A LOT.
YOURS,
NORDLEBERT
```

Type NEW, and write a letter of your own. Here's some space for your creation:

```
100 ______________________________________________
110 ______________________________________________
120 ______________________________________________
130 ______________________________________________
140 ______________________________________________
150 ______________________________________________
160 ______________________________________________
```

Here's a short program that does a lot:

```
10 A: $A = ICE CREAM, YOU SCREAM, WE ALL SCREAM
FOR
20 T: $A $A $A
```

What does this program do? The sentence is a strange one. It could continue forever. You see:

```
ICE CREAM, YOU SCREAM, WE ALL SCREAM FOR ICE
CREAM, YOU SCREAM,
WE ALL SCREAM FOR ICE CREAM, YOU SCREAM, WE ALL
SCREAM FOR
```

MORE ANSWERING SERVICE

The answering service does some more jobs. You can tell the answering service to accept messages by name in the middle of a program. Here is an example:

```
10 T: WHAT'S YOUR NAME?
20 A: $WHO          ACCEPT A STRING CALLED $WHO
30 T: HI THERE $WHO
RUN
```

When you RUN this program, the typer types

WHAT'S YOUR NAME?

Next, the computer stops at line 20 and waits to accept what you type. The message string that you type is stored under the name $WHO. You type your name:

THUMBULBA DURDLEBLUMPST   [RETURN]

The computer goes to line 30, and the typer types:

HI THERE THUMBULBA DURDLEBLUMPST

Here is another example that takes the message you type and then does something with the message. Type NEW and try this:

```
10 T: TYPE SOMETHING, THEN PRESS (RETURN)
20 A: $SOMETHING       ACCEPT A MESSAGE
30 *AGAIN              THIS IS A LABELED LINE
40 , T:$SOMETHING      TYPE THE MESSAGE STRING
50 , J:*AGAIN          JUMP TO *AGAIN
RUN
```

THE MATCHER

There is a matcher in your computer. The matcher checks to see if one word or sentence matches another word or sentence. You can use the matcher to check if answers are correct, or to find particular answers received by the answering service. If the matcher finds a match, it sends the answer Y. Y stands for YES. If the matcher doesn't find a match, it sends the answer N. N stands for NO. The typer and other computer objects can use the Y or the N to decide what to do. The command that calls the matcher to work is M:. Here is an example of the match command M: and Y and N at work:

```
10 T: WHAT COLOR IS A SUNSET?
20 A:           ACCEPT AN ANSWER
30 M: RED           MATCH TO SEE IF THE ANSWER IS RED
40 TY: YES. IT'S BEAUTIFUL           TYPE THIS IF YES
50 TN: I THOUGHT IT WAS RED           TYPE THIS IF NO
RUN
```

When you RUN this program, the typer types

WHAT COLOR IS A SUNSET?

Then, line 20 commands the computer to stop and accept what you type. Next, at line 30, the computer matches what you type against the word RED. Is your answer RED, or not? If the answer is yes, then the typer will type

YES, IT'S BEAUTIFUL

If the answer is no, then the typer will type

I THOUGHT IT WAS RED

In the last example you learned four new, related commands:

A: This commands the answering service to accept an answer.

M: This commands the matcher to match for a specific answer.

TY: The Y controls the typer. The typer types only if the answer matched the specified answer.

TN: The N controls the typer. The typer types only if the answer doesn't match the specified answer.

Here's another example that asks a riddle and checks the answer:

```
10 T: WHAT GOES UP, BUT NEVER COMES DOWN?
20 A:            ACCEPT AN ANSWER
30 M: YOUR AGE            MATCH THIS ANSWER
40 TY: VERY GOOD          TYPE IF THERE'S A MATCH
50 TN: YOUR AGE           TYPE IF NO MATCH
```

Write a program that asks the name of the capital of California. The program should run like this:

WHAT IS THE CAPITAL OF CALIFORNIA?   COMPUTER
SACRAMENTO RETURN   YOU
VERY GOOD   THE COMPUTER

Or, in the case of a wrong answer, the program does this:

WHAT IS THE CAPITAL OF CALIFORNIA?   COMPUTER
OMAHA RETURN   YOU
THE ANSWER IS: SACRAMENTO   COMPUTER

Here is some space for your program:

```
10 _______________________________________
20 _______________________________________
30 _______________________________________
40 _______________________________________
50 _______________________________________
```

ANSWER

```
10 T: WHAT IS THE CAPITAL OF CALIFORNIA?
20 A:
30 M: SACRAMENTO
40 TY: VERY GOOD
50 TN: THE ANSWER IS: SACRAMENTO
```

Here is a program that acts smart. The computer tells about color choices.

```
100 T: WHAT IS YOUR NAME?
110 A: $NAME
120 T: WHAT IS YOUR FAVORITE COLOR, $NAME
130 A: $COLOR
140 M: RED
150 TY: RED IS AN ACTIVE COLOR. YOU MUST LIKE
ACTIVITY.
160 M: YELLOW
170 TY: YELLOW IS AN ALERT COLOR. YOU MUST BE
VERY AWARE.
180 M: BLUE
190 TY: BLUE IS A CALM AND THOUGHTFUL COLOR.
YOU MUST LIKE TO THINK.
200 T: $COLOR IS AN INTERESTING CHOICE, $NAME.
```

MANY MATCHES

Some questions have more than one answer. The matcher can check many answers at once. Here is an example in which many answers are matched:

```
10 T: NAME A COMMON HOUSEHOLD PET
20 A:
30 M: DOG, CAT, HAMSTER, RABBIT
40 TY: YES, THAT'S A COMMON PET
50 TN: NOT VERY COMMON
```

The new thing is in line 30, where the answer you type is checked against four different correct answers. Here is what happens when you RUN the program:

First, the computer types

NAME A COMMON HOUSEHOLD PET

Next, the computer stops and accepts the answer that you type. Let's suppose that you typed

CAT   [RETURN]

When you press RETURN , the computer matches your answer against the expected answers DOG, CAT, HAMSTER, RABBIT. Your answer, CAT, matches the word CAT in the list of expected answers. At line 40, the command TY: means TYPE if YES. Yes, there was a match. The typer types:

YES, THAT IS A COMMON PET.

At line 50, the command TN: means TYPE if NO. But the match gave a definite YES. The typer doesn't type anything this time.

Add line 30 to this program so that it gives a smart response to your answers:

```
10 T: TWO DIMES AND A NICKEL MAKE WHAT?
20 A:
30 ______
40 TY: THAT'S RIGHT
50 TN: I DON'T THINK SO
```

ANSWER: Here's one possibility. Your's might be different. That's ok.

30 M: 25, 25 CENTS, A QUARTER, TWENTY FIVE CENTS

Write a short program that asks:

DO YOU WANT TO GO?

If you type Y, or YES, or OK, then the computer should type:

THEN GO

Otherwise, the computer should type:

THEN DON'T

Here's space for your program:

```
10 ______________________________
20 ______________________________
30 ______________________________
40 ______________________________
50 ______________________________
```

THE MATCHER'S JOB

The MATCH command M: calls the matcher to work. The matcher does more than just check answers. It searches hard for answers. It might find an answer that you don't expect. Type NEW, and try this program:

```
10 T: TYPE: THE HIPPOPOTAMUS
20 A:
30 M:POP          NO SPACES
40 TY: POP IS IN THE HIPPOPOTAMUS
RUN
```

When you RUN this program, type THE HIPPOPOTAMUS when asked. The matcher is called on line 30. The matcher searches for the letters POP anywhere in HIPPOPOTAMUS. Yes, the letters POP are in HIPPOPOTA-MUS. There is a match. The computer types

POP IS IN THE HIPPOPOTAMUS

How many words can you find that will trigger the typer to type the message POP IS IN THE HIPPOPOTAMUS? Here are three that will work: POPE, POPPY, POPULAR. Can you find any that don't begin with the letter P?

SELF-TEST ON CHAPTER 6

1. The command PA: 60 causes a pause of _______? _______ seconds.
2. What command calls the answering service into action? _______
3. What will this program do?

        10 A:
        20 T: DONE

   ____

4. Message strings can have names. The name of a message string must start with _______? _______.
5. Write a command that stores the message string THIS IS IMPORTANT under the name $IMP.

   ____

6. Finish the following program so that it will type the message GOOD JOB on the screen:

        10 _______________________________________
        20 _______________________________________
        30 T: $A $B

7. What will this program type out?

        10 A: $ZAP = GO FOR A LONG WALK
        20 T: MO, I WANT TO $ZAP WITH YOU.

   ____

8. What will this program do?

        110 A: $NAME
        120 T: $NAME

   ____

9. Add a command at line 20 of the following program so that when you type GOOD, the computer types VERY GOOD.

```
10 A:
20 ________________________________
30 TY: VERY GOOD
```

10. Write a program that accepts an answer, then checks if the answer contains one of the vowels A, E, I, O, or U. If the answer does contain a vowel, then the computer should type VOWEL. If the answer doesn't contain a vowel, then the computer should type NO VOWEL.

ANSWERS:

1. The command PA: 60 causes a pause of 60 jiffies, or 1 second.

2. The command A: calls the answering service into action.

3. The program looks like this:

```
10 A:        THE COMPUTER STOPS AND WAITS FOR
             THE  [RETURN]  KEY
20 T: DONE     WHEN YOU PRESS  [RETURN] , THE
             COMPUTER TYPES THIS
```

4. The names of message strings always start with a $.

5. Here is a command that stores the message string THIS IS IMPORTANT under the name $IMP:

```
A: $IMP = THIS IS IMPORTANT
```

6. Here is a program that will type the message GOOD JOB:

```
10 A: $A = GOOD
20 A: $B = JOB
30 T: $A $B
```

7. The program

```
10 A: $ZAP = GO FOR A LONG WALK
20 T: MO, I WANT TO $ZAP WITH YOU.
```

will type

MO, I WANT TO GO FOR A LONG WALK WITH YOU.

8. The program

```
110 A: $NAME
120 T: $NAME
```

will stop and accept what you type. When you press RETURN , the letters that you type will be typed again.

9. Here is a program that types VERY GOOD when you type GOOD:

```
10 A:
20 M: GOOD
30 TY: VERY GOOD
```

10. Here is a program that checks what you type for vowels:

```
10 A:
20 M:A,E,I,O,U
30 TY: VOWEL
40 TN: NO VOWEL
```

SUMMARY OF CHAPTER 6

In this chapter you learned:

- that there are 60 jiffies to a second
- that PA: 60 causes the computer to pause for 1 second
- that A: causes the answering service to listen for your message
- that messages to the answering service are ended with RETURN
- that message strings can be given names
- that the names of message strings always start with a $
- that the A: command can be used to assign a name to a message string and to store the string
- that message strings can be recalled by name and typed with the command T:
- that message strings can be used to make new message strings
- how to use message strings to make a thank-you letter
- that the match command M: can be used to match accepted answers against expected answers
- that the matcher sends the messages Y and N to other computer objects depending on whether or not a match is found
- that the typer, and other computer objects, are controlled by the messages Y and N sent by the matcher
- that TY: types if the matcher says Y; TN: types if the matcher says N
- that many matches may be made at once
- that the matcher searches to see if the expected answer is hidden in the accepted answer

7

TURTLE MAPS

In this chapter you will learn about turtle maps. Turtle maps help the turtle find out where it is. You can send the turtle anyplace on the screen once you know about the map. In this chapter you will learn:

- that the screen is made up of little squares
- that each square has a two-number address
- that you can tell the graphics turtle to GOTO any address
- that the upper right corner of the screen has address 39, 79
- that the question mark generates random numbers from 0 to 32767
- that the \ operator gives the remainder on division
- that the turtle can DRAWTO any address on the screen
- that the turtle can TURNTO any direction
- that turtle space is bigger than the screen
- that the highest address in turtle space is 32767, 32767
- that the %X and %Y are the names of the turtle's two address numbers
- that %A is the name of the turtle's direction number
- how to herd turtles
- how to fill in areas of color with the FILL command

THE GRAPHICS SCREEN

The turtle moves on the screen. The screen is made up of many little squares. Each square has an address consisting of two numbers. The address of the center of the screen is 0,0.

The square to the right of the center is 1,0. The square to the left of 0,0 is −1,0.

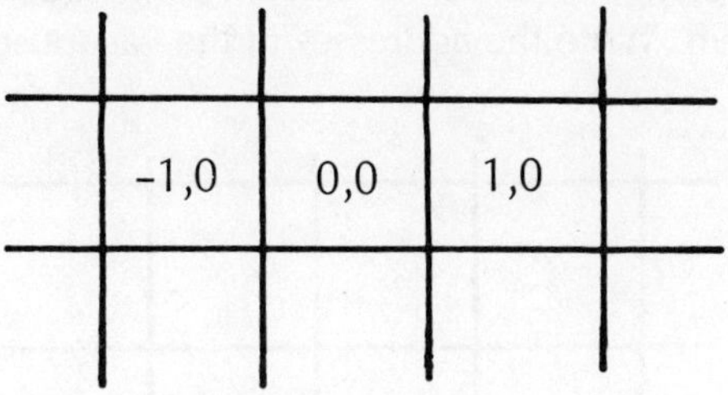

-1,0	0,0	1,0

The square above the center is 0,1. The square below 0,0 is 0,−1.

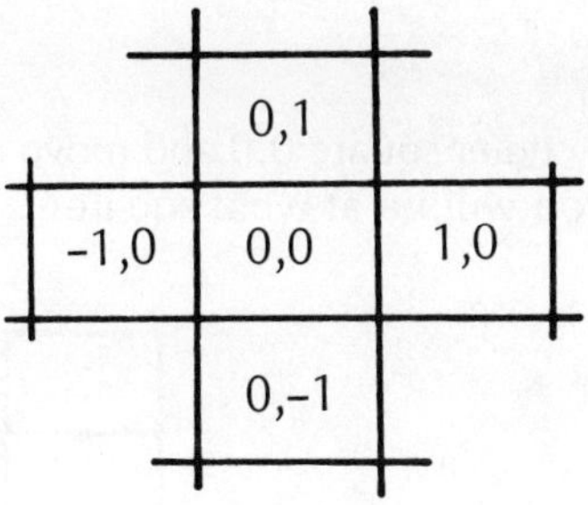

	0,1	
-1,0	0,0	1,0
	0,−1	

If you move to the right and up, you get to the square 1,1.

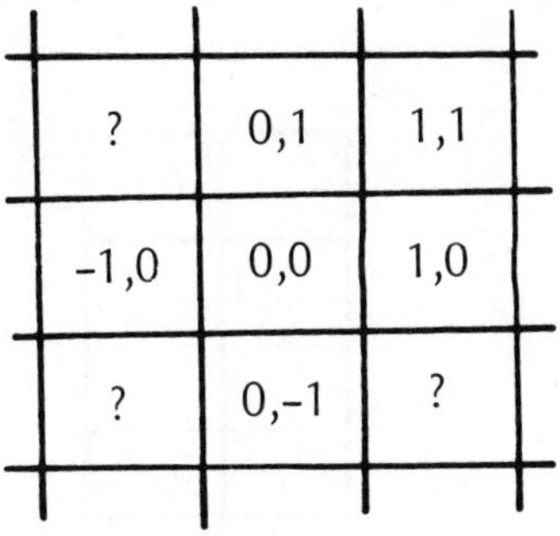

?	0,1	1,1
-1,0	0,0	1,0
?	0,−1	?

Here is a picture of part of the screen. Some squares have their addresses written in them. Write the addresses in the vacant squares.

<table>
<tr><td></td><td>1,2</td><td>2,2</td><td></td><td></td></tr>
<tr><td>0,1</td><td></td><td></td><td>3,1</td><td></td></tr>
<tr><td>0,0</td><td></td><td>2,0</td><td></td><td></td></tr>
</table>

If you start at the center square 0,0 and move right 2 squares, and move up 3 squares, then you will be at what square?

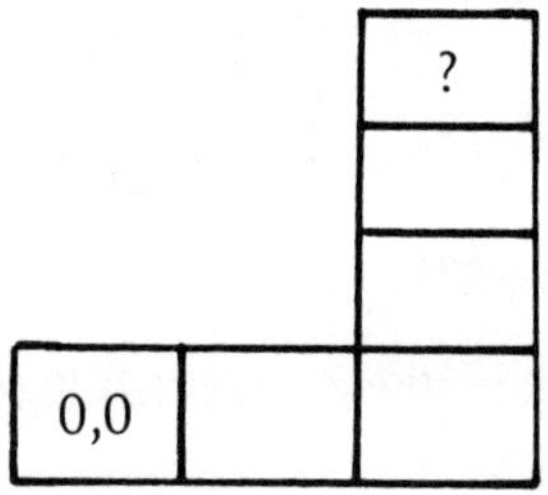

If you start at the center 0,0 and move left 1 and down 3, then you will be at what square?

<table>
<tr><td>-1,0</td><td>0,0</td></tr>
<tr><td>-1,-1</td><td></td></tr>
<tr><td>-1,-2</td><td></td></tr>
<tr><td>?</td><td>0,-3</td></tr>
</table>

ANSWERS:

-3,3	-2,3	-1,3	0,3	1,3	2,3	3,3
-3,2	-2,2	-1,2	0,2	1,2	2,2	3,2
-3,1	-2,1	-1,1	0,1	1,1	2,1	3,1
-3,0	-2,0	-1,0	0,0	1,0	2,0	3,0
-3,-1	-2,-1	-1,-1	0,-1	1,-1	2,-1	3,-1
-3,-2	-2,-2	-1,-2	0,-2	1,-2	2,-2	3,-2
-3,-3	-2,-3	-1,-3	0,-3	1,-3	2,-3	3,-3

GOTO

You can tell the graphics turtle to go immediately to any point on the screen.
The turtle will make a dot when it gets there.

Give this a try:

GR: GOTO 0,0   RETURN

You see this:

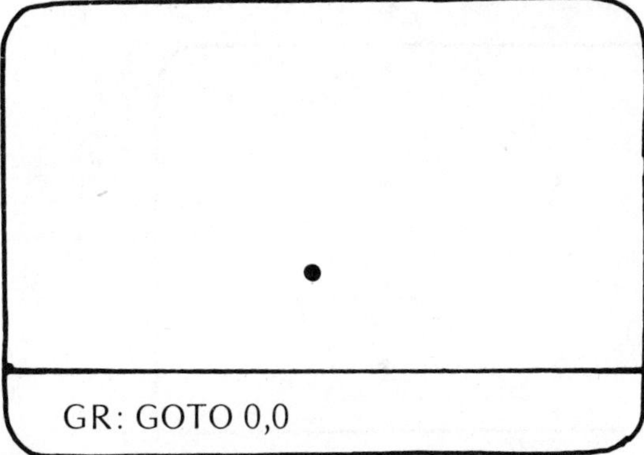

Try this:

GR: GOTO 30, 10   RETURN

You see this:

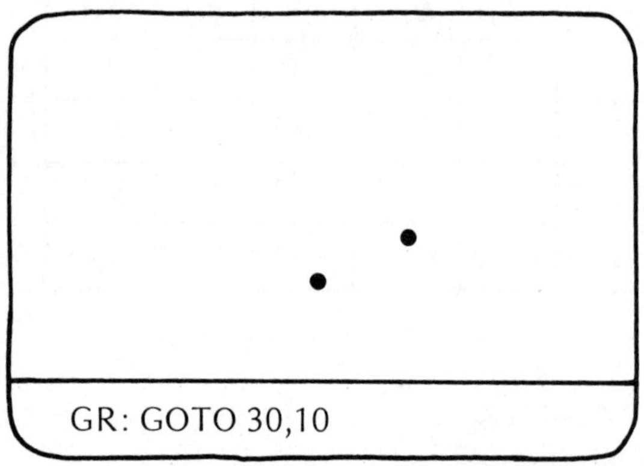

Here is the instruction to make the turtle plot the corners of a tiny square around the center of the screen. Type SHIFT   CLEAR to clear the screen, and give it a try:

GR: GOTO 9,9; GOTO −9,9; GOTO −9,−9; GOTO 9,−9
RETURN

You see this:

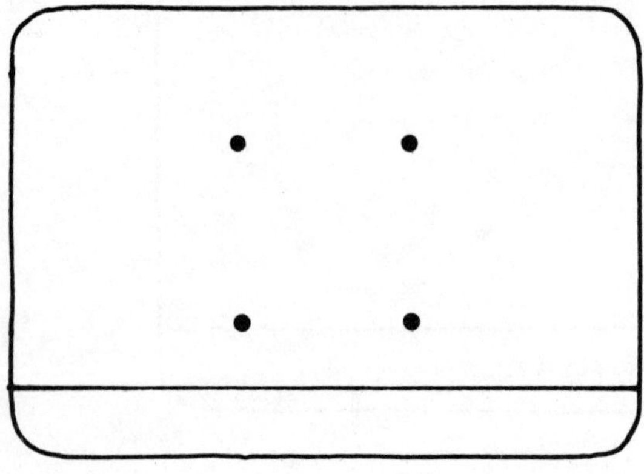

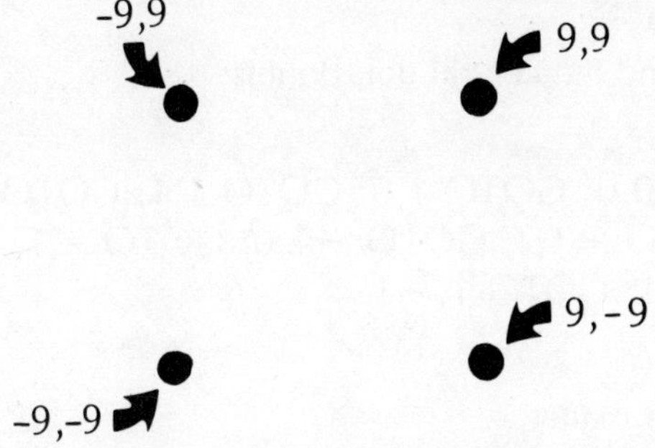

Here's something for you to do. Put dots all around the central dot, like this:

-1,1	0,1	1,1
-1,0	0,0	1,0
-1,-1	0,-1	1,-1

Here's the command that puts a dot at the right side of the screen:

GR: GOTO 79,0

Put a dot at the far left side of the screen.
Here's the command that put's a dot at the top of the screen:

GR: GOTO 0,39

Put a dot at the bottom of the screen. Be careful, you'll need to experiment. The text area blocks part of the screen. Find the dot in the middle, just above the text area.
Put a dot in the upper right-hand corner of the screen.

ANSWERS:

To put dots around the central dot, do this:

```
GR: GOTO 0,0; GOTO 1,0; GOTO 1,1; GOTO 0,1; GOTO
-1,1; GOTO -1,1; GOTO -1,0; GOTO -1,-1;
GOTO 0,-1; GOTO 1,-1
```

The order doesn't matter.
   To put a dot at the far left do this:

```
GR: GOTO -79,0
```

To put a dot at the bottom just above the text area, do this:

```
GR: 0,-31
```

To put a dot in the upper right-hand corner, do this:

```
GR: GOTO 79,39
```

THE GRAPHICS SCREEN

Here is a picture of the graphics screen:

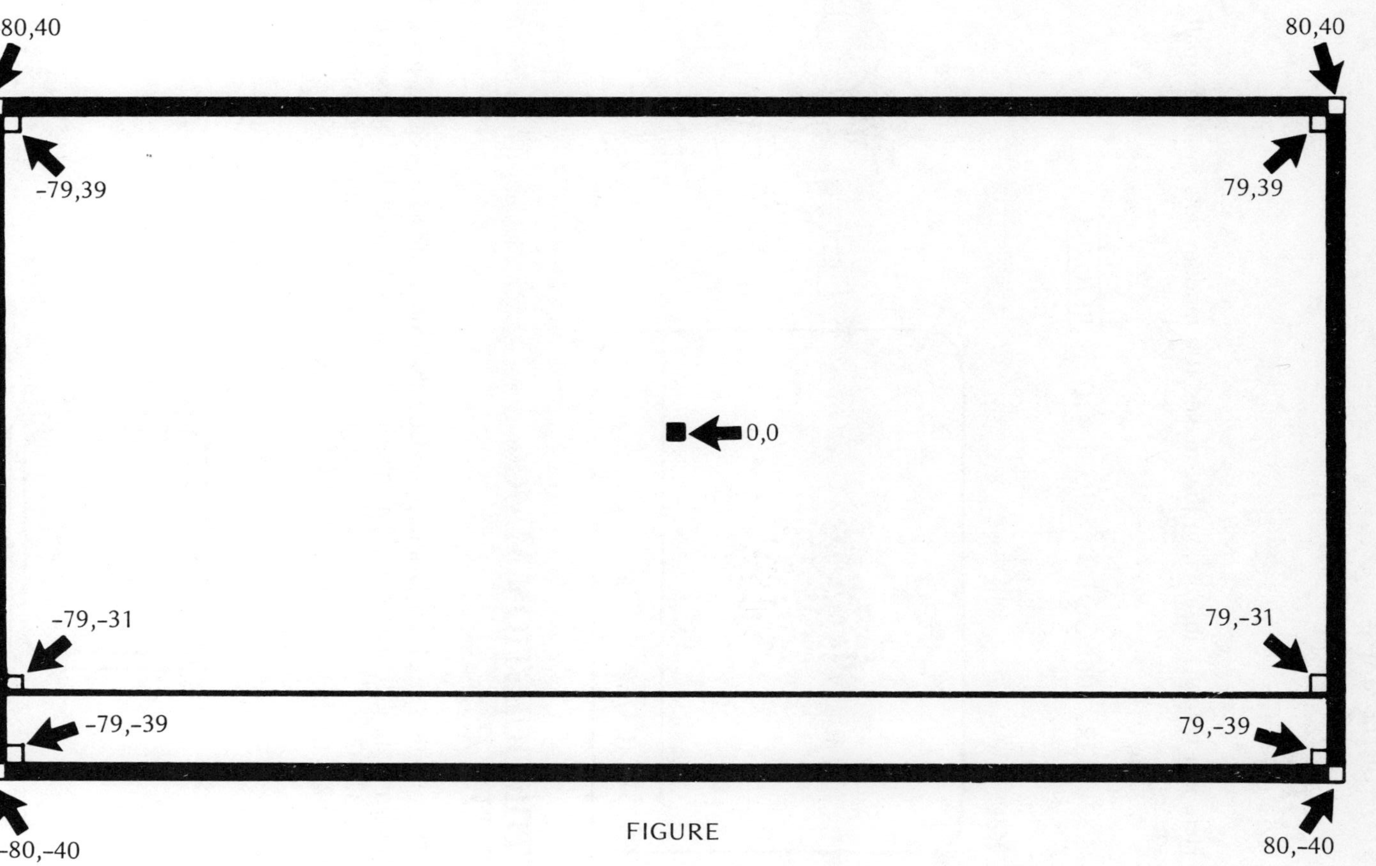

FIGURE

DOTS

Here is a graphics instruction that makes 100 random dots inside a small square:

GR: 100(GOTO ?\10, ?\10)   RETURN

You see this:

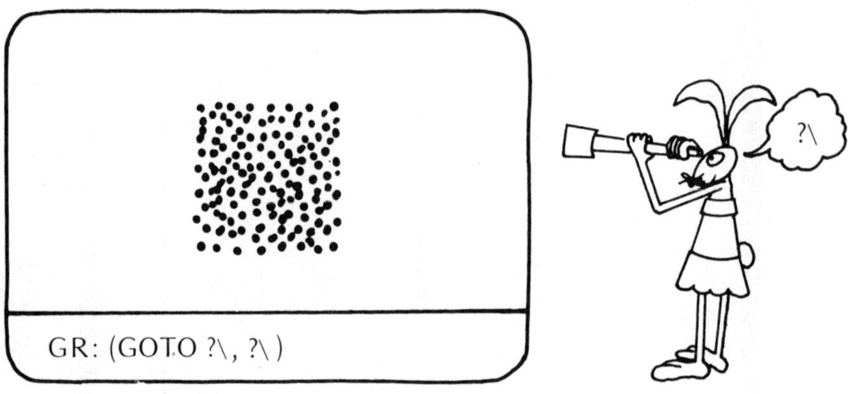

THE QUESTION MARK

The question mark (?) is interpreted by the computer as a request for a random number. The computer obediently chooses a number between 0 and 32767 and puts the number in place of the question mark. The number 32767 is the biggest number that PILOT can handle.

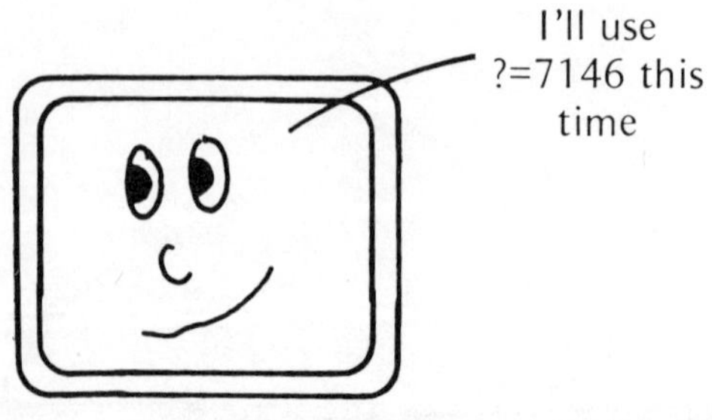

Change the previous command so that it looks like this:

    GR: 100(GOTO ?\60, ?\30)

You see this:

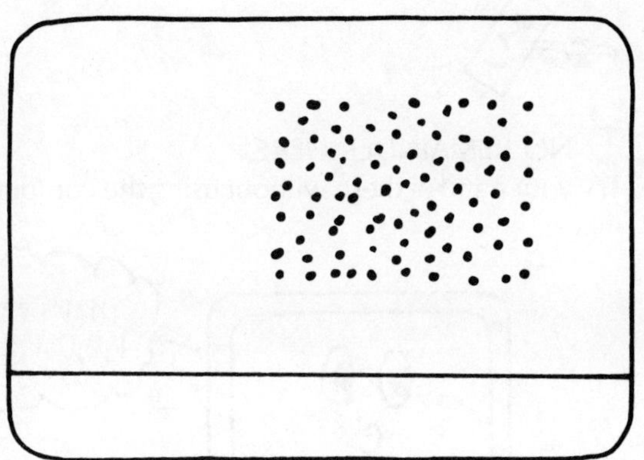

THE NUMBER CHOPPER \

When you have some big numbers that you want to make small, the number
chopper '\' is just what you need. It is also called the backslash. The '\'
looks a lot like the division sign '/'. But, \ is not /. The backslash operator
gives you the remainder on division. It tells you what number is left over
after dividing one number by another. You will use \ a lot.

Here is an example:

3\2 = 1  WHEN 3 IS DIVIDED BY 2,
THE REMAINDER IS 1.

$$2)\overline{\begin{array}{c}1\\3\\\underline{2}\\1\end{array}}$$

What is 4\2? NO REMAINDER HERE.
Here are a few more. Try your hand at these without using the computer.

1\3 =
2\3 =
3\3 =
4\3 =
5\3 =
6\3 =
3001\3 =

Here's a question about the number chopper and the question mark:

?\10 = — — — — — — — — — — —

What numbers might this give?

?\10 yields the numbers
0,1,2,3,4,5,6,7,8,9
chosen at random.

What numbers might these give?

?\2 = — —
?\3 = ______
?\6 = ______
?\6 + 1 = ______

ANSWERS: 0,1; 0,1,2; 0,1,2,3,4,5; 1,2,3,4,5,6

Can you guess what this will do? Try it.

GR: 100(GOTO ?\60, 0)

You see this:

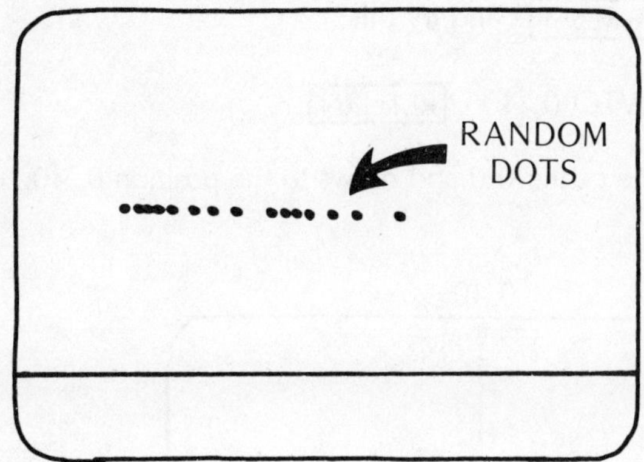

DRAWTO

The DRAWTO command is similar to the DRAW command. The DRAWTO command tells the turtle to draw as it goes to a place on the screen. Press SYSTEM RESET and give this a try:

GR: DRAWTO 20, 10 RETURN

The turtle starts at the center of the screen, and then draws to the position 20, 10. You see this:

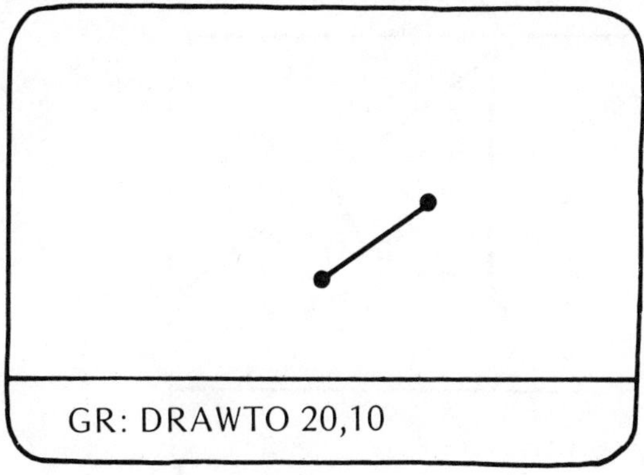

DRAWTO is different from DRAW.

GR: DRAW 20 DRAW STRAIGHT AHEAD 20 STEPS, 10
GR: DRAWTO 20, 10 DRAW ON THE WAY TO 20, 10

Press SYSTEM RESET and try this:

GR: DRAWTO 0, 40   RETURN

The turtle starts at the center 0,0 and draws to the position 0, 40. You see this:

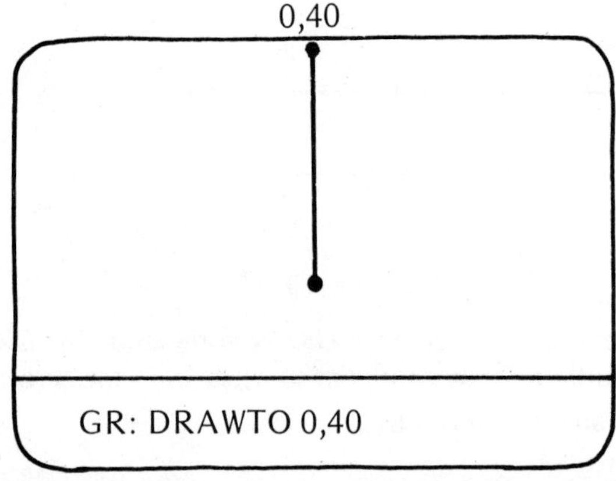

Write the command that will draw a RED line from the turtle's present position (0, 40) to the position 80, 0. The screen should look like this:

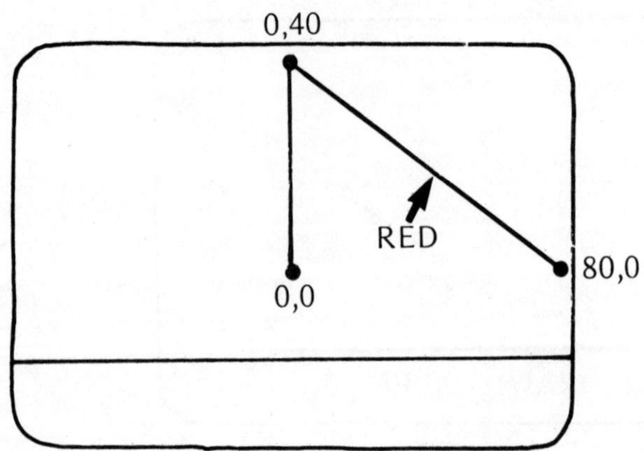

Now give the command that draws a blue line from the position 80, 0 to the position 0,0.

ANSWERS:

GR: PEN RED; DRAWTO 80, 0
GR: PEN BLUE; DRAWTO 0, 0

Here is a command that uses the whole screen. Type

[SYSTEM RESET]

and give it a try:

REPEAT
1000 TIMES

$$-80 \text{ to } 79 \quad -40 \text{ to } 39$$

GR: 1000(DRAWTO ?\160-80, ?\80-40)   [RETURN]

AXIS

Here is a program module called *AXIS which draws horizontal and vertical lines through the center of the screen:

100 *AXIS
110 , GR: CLEAR 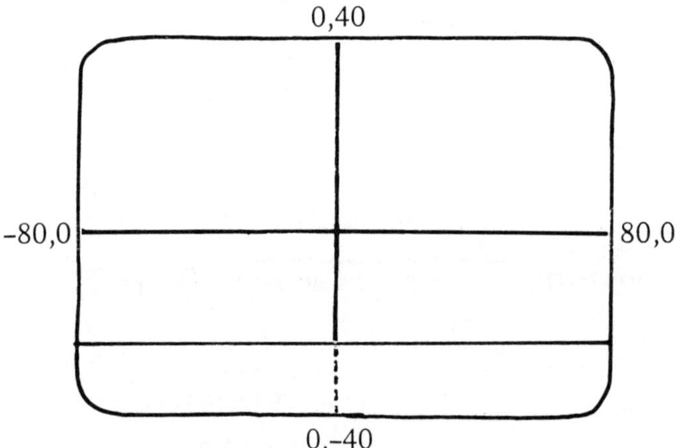 CLEAR THE SCREEN
120 , GR: GOTO − 80, 0 GO TO LEFT CENTER
130 , GR: DRAWTO 80, 0 DRAW TO THE RIGHT
140 , GR: GOTO 0, − 40 GO TO BOTTOM CENTER
150 , GR: DRAWTO 0, 40 DRAW TO TOP CENTER
160 , GR: GOTO 0, 0 RETURN TURTLE TO CENTER
170 , E: END OF MODULE

Remember the PEN ERASE command? Use it to take a point out of the horizontal line at the position 10, 0.

ANSWER :

GR: PEN ERASE; GOTO 10,0

TURNTO

You can tell the turtle to turn and point in any direction. The turtle's screen compass looks like this:

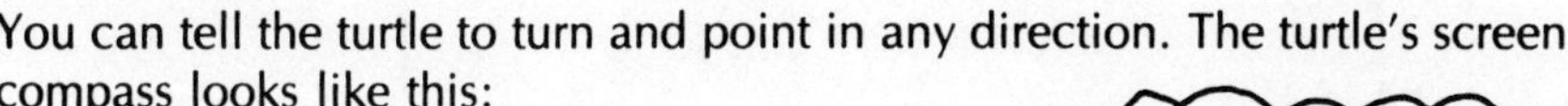

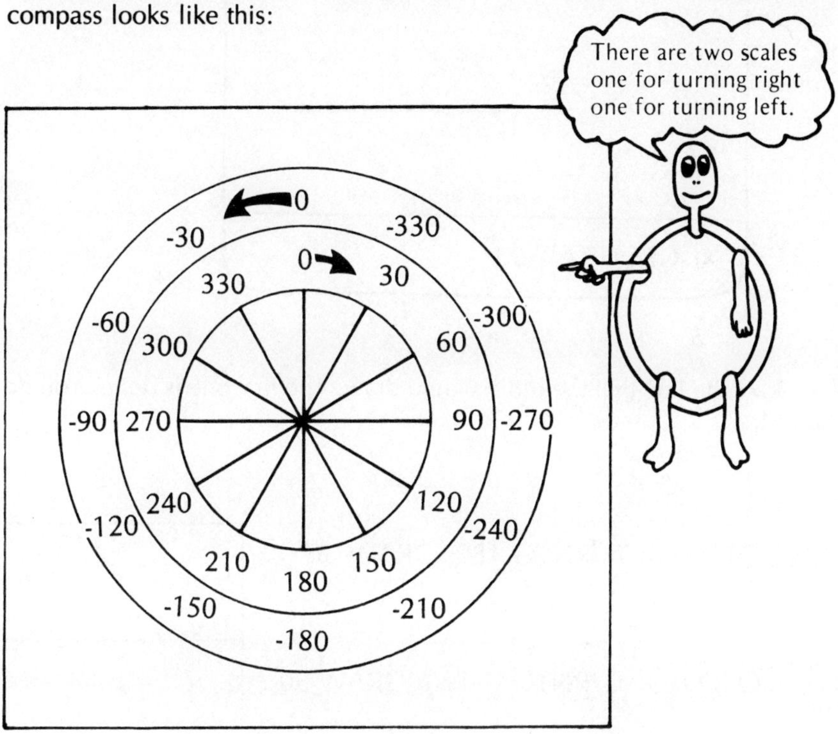

Press   SYSTEM RESET   and try this:

GR: TURNTO 90   RETURN

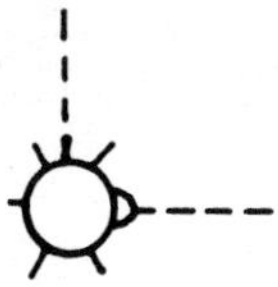

The turtle has turned to face toward the right side of the screen. You can't see the turtle because it is invisible.

Check the turtle's direction by telling it to draw:

GR: DRAW 50

You see this:

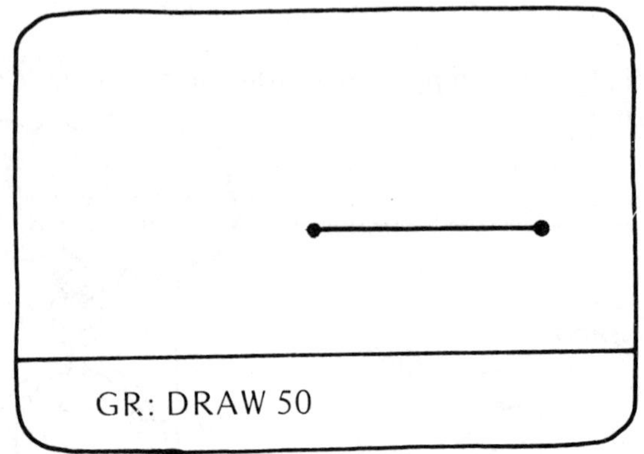

Draw the line that the turtle would draw. The first one is done. You do the rest.

GR: GOTO 0,0; TURNTO 180; DRAW 30

GR: GOTO 0,0; TURNTO −120; DRAW 30

GR: GOTO 0,0; TURNTO 30; DRAW 30

GR: GOTO 0,0; TURNTO −30; DRAW 30

ANSWERS:

Press   SYSTEM RESET   and give this a try:

GR: 100(GOTO 0,0; TURNTO ?; DRAW ?\30)

You see this:

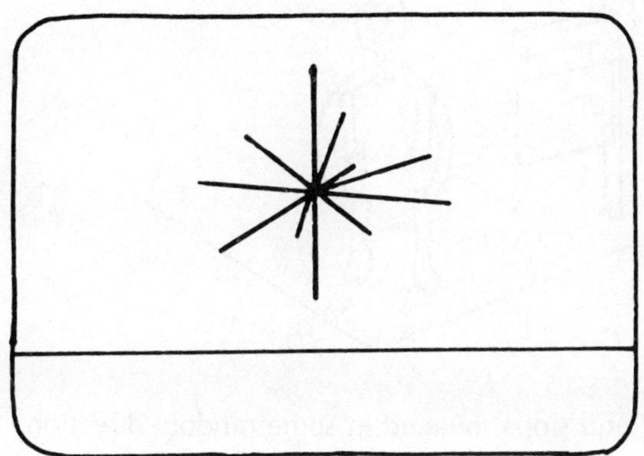

TURTLE SENSE

Turtles have a marvelous sense of direction. A turtle can navigate thousands of miles to find its way home. The graphics turtle shares the good navigating sense of its oceangoing relatives. The graphics turtle can sense its exact screen position and the direction in which it is heading.

Press   SYSTEM RESET   and try this:

GR: GOTO ?, ? ; TURNTO ?   RETURN

The turtle runs off into turtle space. Here is the picture of the signpost at the center of turtle space:

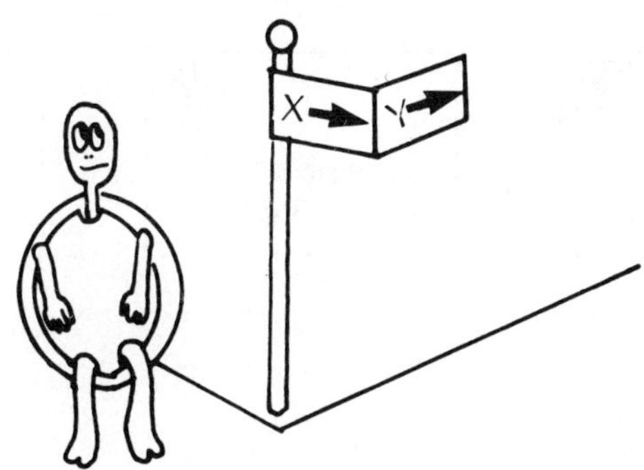

The turtle finds a spot in turtle space.

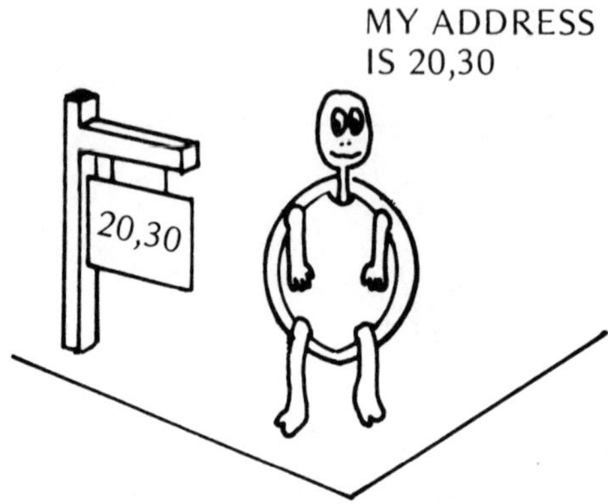

Turtle spins around and stops, headed in some random direction.

Turtle sends three messages that reveal its location.
The names of the three messages are %X, %Y, and %A.

Remember that places in turtle space have addresses. The addresses are pairs of numbers like

8, 12

or even

32767, 32767

%X and %Y bring the address of the turtle.
%A brings the direction number of the turtle.

The typer can type the address numbers for you. Try this:

T: %X, %Y   RETURN

We got

1732, 341

for our turtle's position. You will probably get something else for your turtle's position.

The typer can also type the direction number of the turtle. Try this:

T: %A

You see some number between 0 and 360. Here is what we got for our turtle:

47

Here is a short puzzle: What will this print on the screen?

```
1 GR: GOTO 100, 200; TURN 180
2 T: %X, %Y, %A
RUN
```

Here is a program. When you type the RETURN key, the turtle goes to a random spot on the screen and points in a random direction. The typer tells you where the turtle is and how it is headed.

    100 *HIDE
    110 , A: 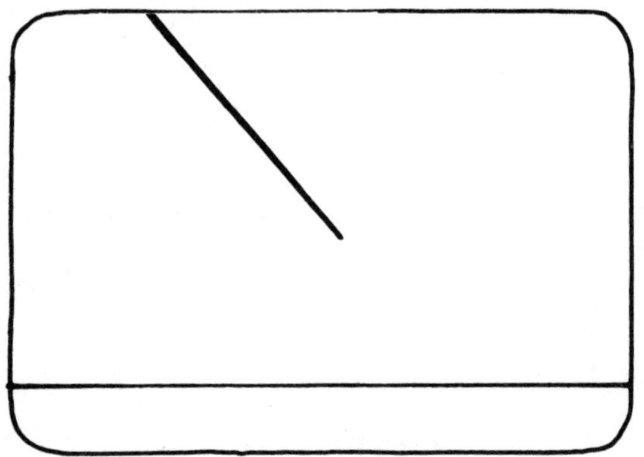 WAIT FOR THE RETURN   KEY
    120 , GR: DRAWTO ?, ?; TURNTO ?   RANDOM
                                    POSITION AND DIRECTION
    130 , T: %X %Y %A   TELL POSITION AND
                                    DIRECTION
    140 , J: *HIDE   JUMP TO *HIDE
    RUN

You see something like this after pressing RETURN   once:

The turtle is probably off the screen into turtle space. You can't see what the turtle does there, but you know where the turtle is and in which direction the turtle is headed.

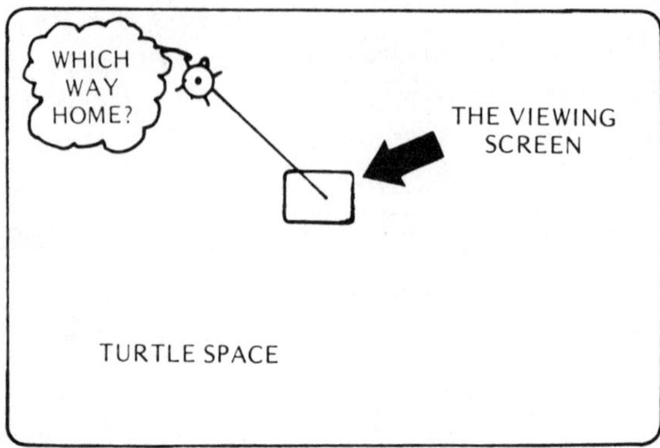

TURTLE HERDER

Here is where you learn how to herd turtles. This next program sends the turtle off to the wilds. Your job is to herd the turtle back. How long will it take you to get the turtle home to 0,0?

```
100 *HERDER
110 , GR: GOTO ?, ?; TURNTO ?        ☞  RANDOM
120 , *NEXT  ☞  YOU'LL RETURN TO THIS LINE
130 , T: THE TURTLE IS AT %X, %Y AND HEADED %A

140 , A:  ☞  WAIT FOR THE  [RETURN]  KEY
150 , T: HOW MUCH SHOULD THE TURTLE TURN?
160 , A: #T  ☞  ACCEPT A NUMBER, CALL IT #T

170 , T: HOW FAR SHOULD THE TURTLE GO?
180 , A: #G  ☞  ACCEPT A NUMBER, CALL IT #G

190 , GR: TURN #T; GO #G  ☞  MOVE THE TURTLE

200 , J: *NEXT  ☞  GO DO IT AGAIN
RUN
```

You probably won't see the turtle for a while. Good luck on your turtle herding.

FILL-ER-UP

It is time for something new. Press [SYSTEM RESET] and type NEW. Would you like a wider brush to paint with? Of course you would. Splash around with this one:

```
GR: FILL 10  [RETURN]
```

You see this:

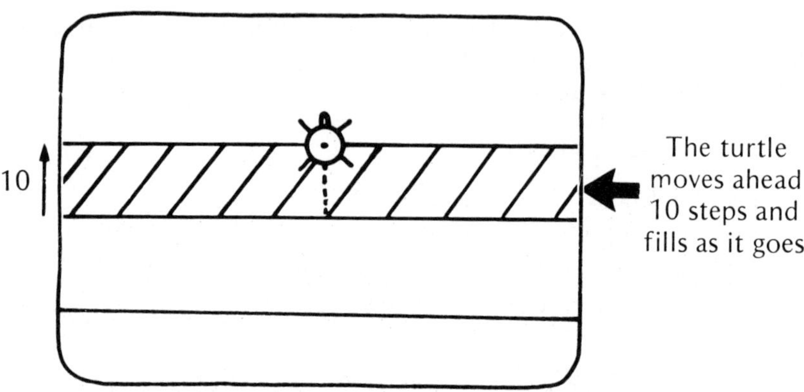

The FILL command tells the turtle to fill in with color as it goes. The turtle went straight ahead 10 steps and filled in as it went.

Try this variation:

GR: GO 5; FILL 5   [RETURN]

You see this:

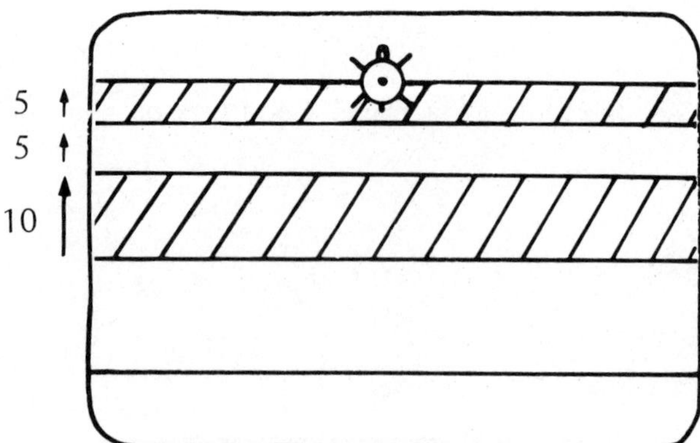

The turtle can fill while moving backwards. Try this:

GR: FILL −40

FANTASY WITH STRIPES

Let's do a lot of something. Press SYSTEM RESET and try this:

```
                          REPEAT
            BOTTOM MIDDLE  40 TIMES
                 ↓        ┌
    10 GR: GOTO 0,  −40; 40(FILL 1; GO 1)
    RUN
```

You see something like this:

Press SYSTEM RESET and add this line to your program:

```
             STARTS ONE
             LINE HIGHER
                 ↓
    20 GR: GOTO 0, −39; 40(FILL 1; GO 1)
    RUN
```

This fills in the remaining stripes.

Add this line to the program:

```
    15 GR: PEN RED
    RUN
```

If you have a color monitor, you see some lovely RED stripes.

BLOCKING THE FILL

The fill proceeds to the right until it is blocked by some previously colored region. If nothing blocks the fill, then it keeps going off the right side of the screen. The fill keeps going and magically reappears from the left side of the screen.

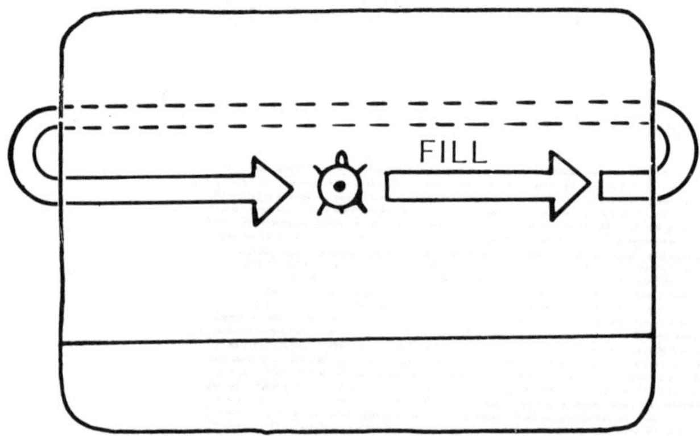

You can see what happens when the fill is blocked by a previously colored region by drawing a barrier line and then doing a fill.

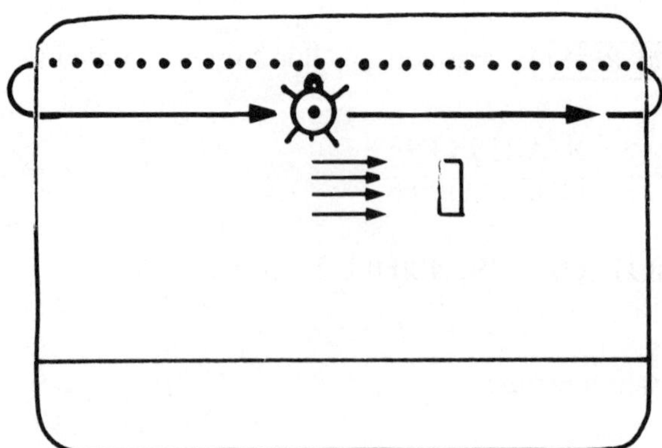

Type NEW and try this:

```
10 GR: GOTO 20,0; DRAW 10
20 GR: GOTO 0,0; FILL 20
```

Here is what you see when you RUN this program:

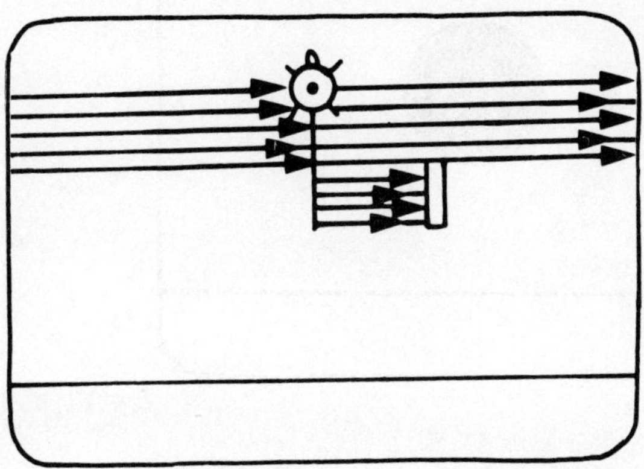

The turtle moves ahead, filling lines out to the right as it goes. The turtle fills each line until it runs into some previously colored region. Then the turtle goes ahead one step and fills to the right again.

Here is a program that fills in a balloon:

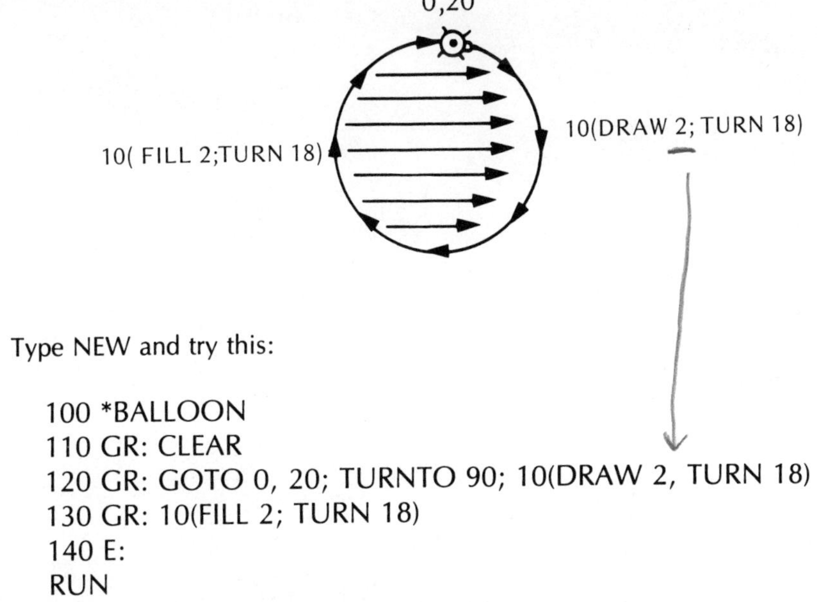

Type NEW and try this:

```
100 *BALLOON
110 GR: CLEAR
120 GR: GOTO 0, 20; TURNTO 90; 10(DRAW 2, TURN 18)
130 GR: 10(FILL 2; TURN 18)
140 E:
RUN
```

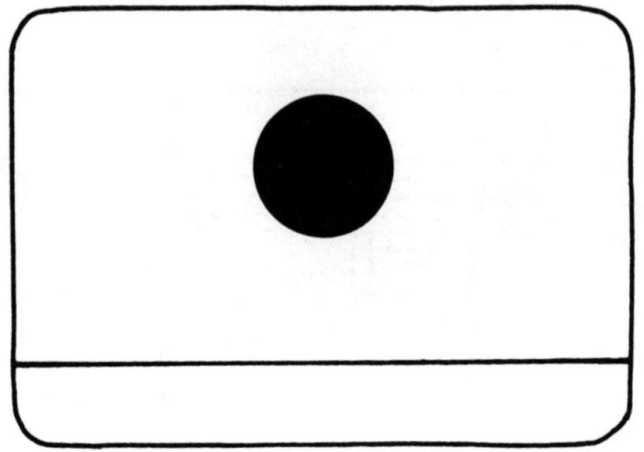

SELF-TEST ON CHAPTER 7

1. What is the address of the center of the screen? _______

2. Where will the turtle be after this command?

    GR: GOTO 39, 79

    ____

3. What is the turtle's direction number when it is facing the top of the screen?

4. Describe how the turtle will be headed when its direction number is 180.

    ____

5. What is 7\3? _______

6. Write the command that draws a line from the center of the screen to the upper right-hand corner.

    ____

7. If the turtle is lost someplace in turtle space, what can you type to find its position?

    ____

8. When the turtle is facing the bottom of the screen, what will this command print on the screen?

    T: %A

    ____

9. Write a command that will send the turtle off to a random position in turtle space.

    ____

10. What is the biggest number in the PILOT language? _______

ANSWERS:

1. The address of the center of the screen is 0, 0.

2. After the command GR: GOTO 39, 79 the turtle will be in the upper right-hand corner of the screen.

3. When the turtle is facing the top of the screen, its direction number is 0.

4. When the turtle's direction number is 180, the turtle is facing the bottom of the screen.

5. The backslash ($\setminus$) gives the remainder on division. The remainder of 7 divided by 3 is $7\setminus3 = 1$.

6. Here is a command that draws a line from the center of the screen to the upper right-hand corner of the screen:

   GR: GOTO 0, 0; DRAWTO 39, 79

7. To find the position of the turtle, type this:

   T: %X, %Y

   The typer will type the two address numbers.

8. When the turtle is facing the bottom of the screen, the command

   T: %A

   will type the direction number

   180

9. Here is one command that will send the turtle off to a random position in turtle space:

   GR: GOTO ?,?

10. The biggest number that you can use in PILOT is 32767.

SUMMARY OF CHAPTER 7

In this chapter you learned:

- that the screen is divided into squares
- that 0,0 is the address of the center of the screen
- that 40,80 is the location just outside the upper right corner
- that you can tell the turtle to GOTO any position in turtle space
- that the far corner of turtle space is at location 32767, 32767
- that the question mark (?) tells the computer to choose a number
- that the question mark is a number between 0 and 32767
- that the backslash (\) gives the remainder on division
- that the question mark and the backslash can make random numbers
- that the turtle can DRAWTO any address
- that the turtle can TURNTO any direction
- that the turtle's position is given by the special numbers %X and %Y
- that the turtle's direction number is given by %A
- how to fill areas with color using the FILL command

HOW TO COMPUTE 8

One of the better things that computers do is work with numbers. This chapter is about numbers and how you can use them to control what the computer does. In this chapter you will learn:

- how to name numbers
- how to call the calculator to do its job
- how to use the calculator to guide the turtle
- how to make gamemasters' dice
- a secret about what happens when you roll three six-sided dice
- about coin matching
- about wandering
- how to make some flashy animated designs

NUMBERS

You have already met some of the computer objects that make up the PILOT language. You have met the typer, the answering service, and the matcher. In this chapter you will meet the calculator. The calculator can add, subtract, multiply, and divide. Before you call the calculator, you need some numbers for it to work on. The chief thing you need to know is that numbers have names. Here are some typical number names:

#N, #A, #X   ⟵— NAMES FOR NUMBERS

In PILOT, the name of a number is made by typing # followed by one of the letters of the alphabet.

THE CALCULATE COMMAND C:

The command C: calls the calculator to do some number work.
   Give this a try:

```
10 C: #N = 12
20 T:#N
RUN
```

You see this:

```
12

READY
□
```

The calculator gives the name #N to the number 12. Next, the typer types out the number stored under the name #N.

SOME ARITHMETIC

Give this a try:

```
10 C: #A = 2 * 3 + 4       THE RESULT IS STORED AS #A
20 T: #A       TYPE NUMBER #A
RUN
```

This is what you see:

```
 10

 READY
```

The calculator does the arithmetic and stores the result under the name #A. The calculator does the arithmetic in a particular order. It works from left to right.

$$\overset{\overset{\displaystyle 10}{\frown}}{\underset{\underset{\displaystyle 6}{\frown}}{\text{C: \#A = 2 * 3 + 4}}}$$

If you want to do the arithmetic in some other order, then you can use parentheses to tell the calculator the proper order.

Change line 10 to this:

```
10 C: #A = 2 * (3 + 4)
```

Here is what you see when you run the program now:

```
14

READY
□
```

The number 2 is multiplied by the number 7. The value stored as #A is the number 14.

In PILOT, all arithmetic is done left to right, unless parentheses are used to change the order.

What does the program type if you change line 10 to this:

```
10 C: #A = 2 + 3 * 4
```

The calculator does the arithmetic from left to right. The number 2 is added to 3, then the result is multiplied by 4. The result is 20. You see this:

```
20

READY
□
```

The calculator can divide. Change line 10 to this:

```
10 C: #A = 6/2
```

The calculator divides 6 by 2. When you RUN the program, you see this:

```
3

READY
□
```

Now that you and your computer can add, how about some addition practice.

Here is a short program that prints out addition problems. Type NEW and give it a try:

```
10 *TOP
20 , C: #A = ?\10
30 , C: #B = ?\10
40 , T: #A + #B = ?
50 , A:
60 , J:*TOP
RUN
```

Here is what we saw when we ran this program:

```
7 + 0 = ?
```

When we pressed RETURN we got a new problem to do. When you are done using the program, press SYSTEM RESET .

If you want some harder problems, change lines 20 and 30 to this:

```
20 , CL #A = ?\100
30 , C: #B = ?\100
```

Now you get two-digit addition problems.

MORE ABOUT / AND \

What is 7 divided by 3? Scribble your answer here: _______

There are at least four ways to answer the previous question. It is really not simple at all.

Answer 1: 7 divided by 3 equals 2.
Answer 2: 7 divided by 3 equals 2 with a remainder of 1.
Answer 3: 7 divided by 3 equals 2 1/3.
Answer 4: 7 divided by 3 equals 2.33333.

In PILOT, the first answer is the correct one.

$$7/3 = 2$$

But that's only half of the story. The other half of the story is this:

$$7 \backslash 3 = 1$$

Did you notice the difference between / and $\backslash$? The $\backslash$ is our old friend the number chopper, alias backslash, alias the remainder.

Quick now, if you have 93 gobs of gum, and 36 eager chewers, then how many pieces of gum will each eager chewer get? How many pieces of gum will be left over? This looks like something the calculator can do.

Here is a program that answers the question about 93 pieces of gum and 36 gum chewers. Type NEW and give it a try.

```
200 C: #Q=93/36
210 T: EACH PERSON GETS #Q PIECES
220 C: #R=93\36
230 T: THERE ARE #R PIECES LEFT OVER
```

Here is what you see when you RUN this program:

```
EACH PERSON GETS 2 PIECES
THERE ARE 21 PIECES LEFT OVER

READY
□
```

You can make the program work for any numbers. Change the program to look like this:

```
100 *DIVISION
110 , T: NUMERATOR?
120 , A: #N          ACCEPT NUMBER #N
130 , T: DENOMINATOR?
140 , A: #D          ACCEPT NUMBER #D

200 , C: #Q=#N/#D       NAME THE QUOTIENT #Q
210 T: EACH PERSON GETS #Q PIECES

220 , C: #R=#N\#D       NAME THE REMAINDER #R
230 , T: THERE ARE #R LEFT OVER

240 , J: *DIVISION
```

When you RUN this program, you see

```
NUMERATOR?
```

Type in a number, say 93. When you press RETURN , you see

```
NUMERATOR?
93
DENOMINATOR?
```

Type the number 36. When you press [RETURN] , you see:

```
NUMERATOR?
93
DENOMINATOR?
36
EACH PERSON GETS 2 PIECES
THERE ARE 21 PIECES LEFT OVER
NUMERATOR?
```

Here are some problems to do with your new program:
1. If 327 tasty fudge brownies are distributed among 32 hungry monks, then how many will each monk get? How many brown fudgies will be left over?
2. If 13,572 ears of corn are shucked by 317 husky shuckers, then how many ears does each shucker shuck? How many ears are left over?

ANSWERS: 10, 7; 42, 257

TURTLE NUMBERS

Here is a program that allows you to change the numbers that the turtle uses to draw. Type NEW and give it a try:

```
100 *POLY
110 , T: DISTANCE TO DRAW?
120 , A: #D            ACCEPT NUMBER #D
130 , T: ANGLE TO TURN?
140 , A: #A            ACCEPT ANGLE TO TURN

150 , GR: 100( DRAW #D; turn #A )        DRAW AND
                                              TURN
```

When you RUN this program you see this:

```
DISTANCE TO DRAW?
□
```

Type 20 and press RETURN . You see:

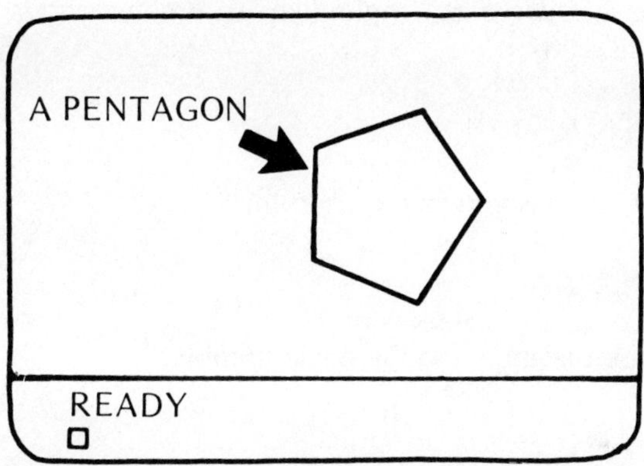

Type 72 and press RETURN . You see this:

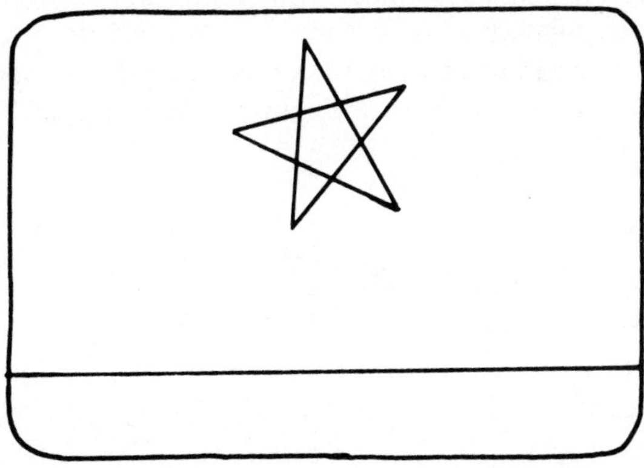

Try these numbers: Use 40 for the distance, and 144 for the angle.

Do each of the following:

> Use 50 for the distance, and 150 for the angle.
>
> Make a triangle.
>
> Make a square.
>
> Make a circle.
>
> Add a graphics command at line 145 to change the pen color
> to red.

Experiment on your own. This program has LOTS of SURPRISES.

ANSWERS: A triangle has angle 120; a square has angle 90; a circle has a short distance, like 4, and a small angle, like 10. A command to change the pen color looks like this:

>   145 GR: PEN RED

Your program deserves some sound. Add this:

>   115 SO: #D, #A

Now you can hear the distance and the angle numbers.

GAMEMASTERS' DICE

If you have ever played a fantasy roleplaying game like Dungeons and Dragons or Runequest, then you know how important it is to have many kinds of dice. You can program your computer to simulate dice and coins. First, let's make the computer act like a coin that comes up 0 or 1.
    Type NEW and try this:

>   100 *TOSS
>   110 , A: WAIT FOR   RETURN
>   120 , C: #D = ?\2   #D EQUALS 0 OR 1
>   130 , T: #D
>   140 , J: *TOSS

Every time you press   RETURN   , the computer tosses the coin. You see either a 0 or a 1. Here is how the screen looks after a few tosses:

```
0
0
1
0
1
1
```

This program is awfully quiet. Let's add some sound. Press BREAK
and type this:

```
113 , SO: 1, 8
115 , PA:20
117 , SO:
```

ONE SIX-SIDED DIE

A minor change in the last program makes it a die thrower. Press BREAK
and change line 120 to this:

```
120 , C: #D = ?\6 + 1        #D EQUALS 1,2,3,4,5,6
```

When you RUN the program, you see something like this:

```
4
5
1
1
6
3
```

A TEN-SIDED DIE

This will be easy. Just change line 120 again:

```
120 , C: #D = ?\10 + 1
```

Change the program so that it throws a twenty-sided die.

120 , ____

ANSWER: 120 C: #D = ?\20 + 1

A GENERAL-PURPOSE DIE

One number in line 120 determines the number of sides on the die.

You can make a general-purpose die with variable sides. Press BREAK , type NEW, and try this:

```
100 *TOSS
110 T:SIDES
120 A: #S            ACCEPT THE NUMBER #S OF SIDES
130 , C: #D = ?\#S + 1
140 , T: ROLL #D
150 , J: *TOSS
```

You can type the number of sides before you call for a toss.

When you run the general-purpose die, the computer stops at line 110 and waits for you to type the number of sides you wish. When you press RETURN , the computer rolls the die.

Use the general-purpose die to roll a 100-sided (decimal) die.

Use the general-purpose die to roll a seven-sided die. Maybe it's a spinner. This might be useful for choosing days of the week at random.

Use the general-purpose die to roll a twelve-sided die. This might be useful for choosing a month of the year or an hour of the day at random.

THRICE DICE

You can make the previous program throw many dice at once. Here is a program that throws three dice, with any number of sides, and adds the total for you. Just add lines 132, 134, 136, and 140 to get this program:

```
100 *TOSS
110 , T:SIDES?
120 , A: #S            ACCEPT THE NUMBER #S OF SIDES
130 , C: #D = ?\#S + 1            THE FIRST DIE
132 , C: #E = ?\#S + 1            THE SECOND DIE
134 , C: #F = ?\#S + 1            THE THIRD DIE
136 , C: #G = #D + #E + #F            THE TOTAL
140 , T:ROLL #G
150 , J: *TOSS
```

There is much to be learned from this program, as you shall see.

Use the three-dice program to throw three six-sided dice. Make a check mark in the proper box below to remember the result:

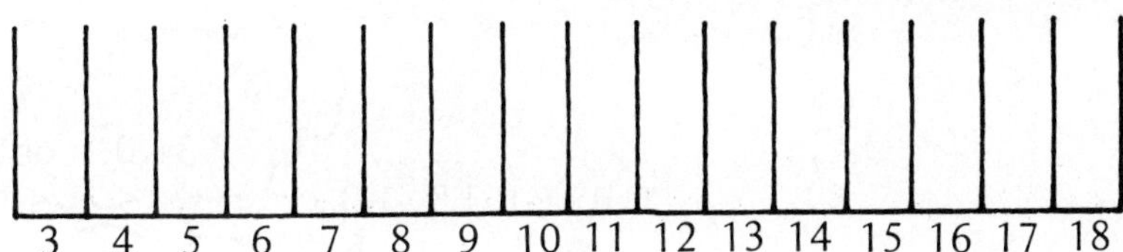

Throw the three dice again—in fact, do it about 20 times. You will learn a very important fact about rolling three six-sided dice.

A SECRET FACT

The numbers you get when you throw three six-sided dice tend to fall between 7 and 14. Your numbers will stack up something like this:

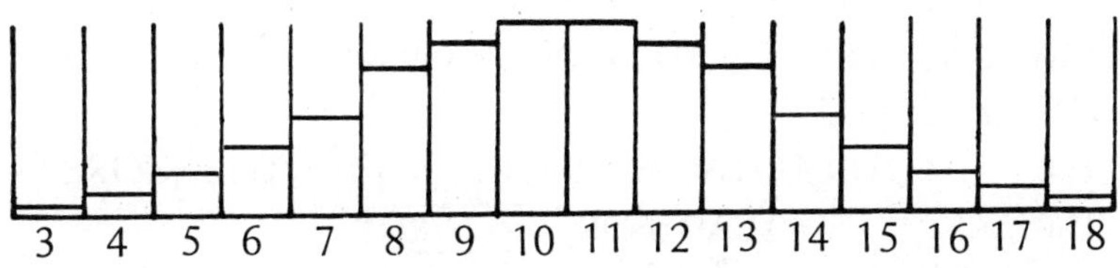

Once you've seen how the numbers stack up, you can predict the outcome with greater precision.

Would you expect to roll a 5 very often using three six-sided dice?

RANDOM WALK

Here is a gambling game. Each time you press [RETURN] you win, tie, or lose the toss of a coin. Your total winnings or losses are shown on the screen. Type NEW and give it a try:

```
100 *GAMBLE
110 , C: #S = 5          YOU START WITH 5 DOLLARS
120 , *TOSS
```

No comma!

THIS GIVES –1,0,1

```
130 , C: #S = #S +(?\3 − 1)
```

NEW #S   OLD #S

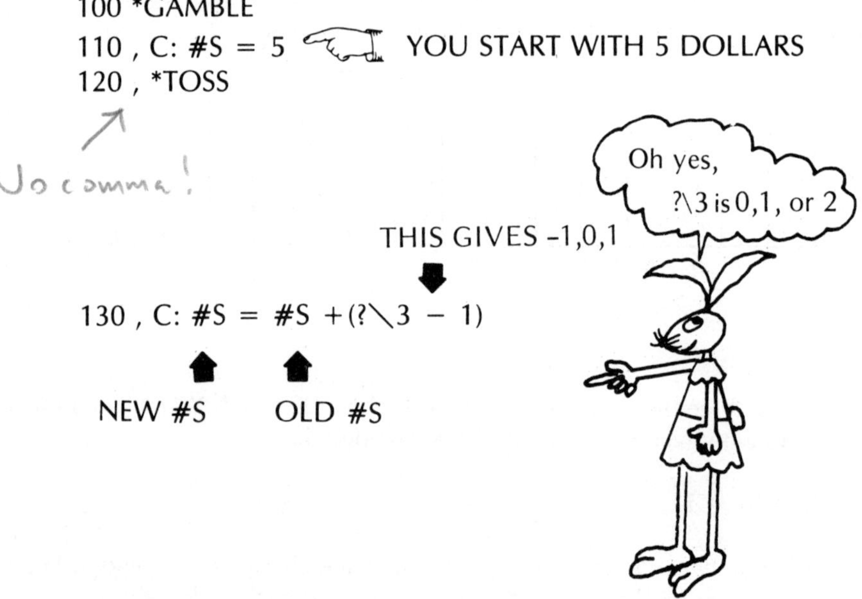


```
140 , GR: CLEAR; GOTO 0,0; DRAW #S        DRAW
LINE #S LONG
150 , T: YOUR TOTAL IS #S        TYPE THE SCORE
160 , A:        WAIT FOR  [RETURN]
170 , J:*TOSS        JUMP TO *TOSS
RUN
```

Here's what you see when you press $\boxed{\text{RETURN}}$:

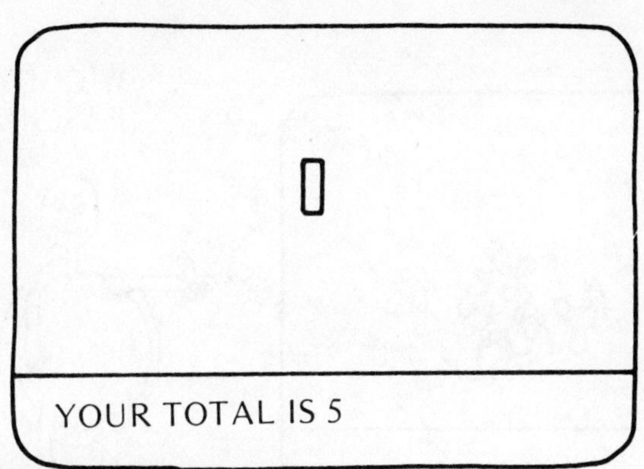

Each time you press $\boxed{\text{RETURN}}$, your new total is displayed. The line in the middle of the screen grows longer or shorter with the total.

Add this to get a sound that goes with your score:

    135 , SO: #S

Add this to get a reference line across the middle of the screen:

    145 GR: GOTO −40,0; DRAWTO 40,0

TURTLE WALK

This next program illustrates wandering. Wandering is a useful thing to do. For one thing, you often wander into something interesting. The turtle wanders well. Type NEW and try this program:

```
100 C: #X = 0        #X and #Y RECORD THE TURTLE'S
                         ADDRESS
110 C: #Y = 0
120 GR: GOTO #X, #Y        THE TURTLE STARTS AT 0,0

130 *WANDER
140 , C: #X = #X +(?\5 − 2)
150 , C: #Y = #Y +(?\5 − 2)
160 , GR: DRAWTO #X, #Y
170 , J:*WANDER
```

When you run this program, you see something like this:

Add some sound.

How long does it take for the turtle to wander off the screen?

165 , SO: #X, #Y

A CALCULATING TURTLE

The turtle can do some flashy tricks with numbers. The calculator can change the numbers that the turtle uses as it goes. Give this a try:

```
100 *SQUARES
110 , C: #X=1           LET #X EQUAL 1
120 , SO: #X            TURN ON SOUND #X
130 , *DRAW
140 , GR: 4(DRAW #X; TURN 90)      A SQUARE
```

150 , C: #X = #X + 1    THE NEW #X IS OLD #X + 1
160 , J: *DRAW   GO DRAW ANOTHER

When you run this program, this is what you see:

The distance that the turtle draws is determined by the number #X. The number #X keeps getting bigger in line 150. The turtle draws a square of side #X. Then, on line 150, the number #X is increased by 1. The turtle draws the square with the bigger value for #X. You see squares that grow and fill the corner of the screen. Press SYSTEM RESET when the drawing is done.

You can make the squares grow faster by changing line 150:

150 , C: #X = #X + 4

Now the side of the square changes faster.

You can make the squares start big and get smaller. Make these changes:

110 , C: #X = 80   THE SIZE OF THE SIDE IS 80
150 , C: #X = #X − 1   #X GETS SMALLER

Now you see squares that start large and decrease in size toward the center.

You can get the appearance of motion if you add this line:

135 GR: CLEAR

Here is a surprising change:

    135 GR: TURN 10
    140 GR: 3(DRAW #X, TURN 120)

Play around. What can you find?

PLAY

SELF-TEST ON CHAPTER **8**

1. Number names always begin with what? _________
2. What will this program type on the screen?

        10 C: #A = 2*3
        20 T: #A

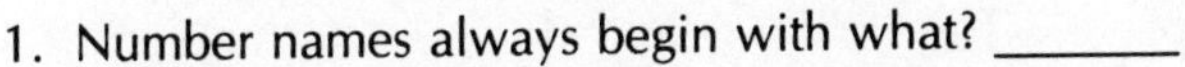

3. What will this program type on the screen?

        10 C: #X = 2 + 3 * 5
        20 T: #X

____

4. What will this program type on the screen?

        10 C: #Y = 5*(1 + 2)
        20 T: #Y

____

5. ?\10 can be what numbers? _________
6. What will this program type on the screen?

        10 C: #Q = 13 /5
        20 T: #Q

7. What will this program type on the screen?

        10 C: #Q = 1 \5
        20 T: #Q

8. Write a PILOT program that accepts a number that you type, and then types twice the number.

10 ____

20 ____

30 ____

9. Describe what this program will type:

```
10 *BEGIN
20 , C: #R = ?\2
30 , T: #R
40 , J: *BEGIN
```

____

10. Write a program that will generate sounds 0 to 9 at random. Each sound should last about 1/6 of a second.

10____

20____

30____

40____

50____

ANSWERS:

1. Number names always begin with #.

2. The program types 6.

3. The program types 25.

4. The program types 15.

5. ?\10 can equal 0,1,2,3,4,5,6,7,8, or 9.

6. The program types 2, since 13 divided by 5 equals 2 plus a remainder.

7. The program types 3, since 13 divided by 5 leaves a remainder of 3.

8. Here is one program that accepts a number, and then types twice the number on the screen.

```
10 A: #N
20 C: #M = 2 * #N
30 T: #M
```

9. The program types the random number #R. #R equals 0 or 1.

10. Here is one program that generates the sounds 0 to 9 at random:

```
10 *TUNE
20 C: #R = ?\10
30 SO:#R
40 PA: 10
50 J:*TUNE
```

SUMMARY OF CHAPTER 8

In this chapter you learned:

- that names of numbers consist of # followed by a single letter
- that the command C: calls the calculator to work
- that C: #N = 12 tells the calculator to give the name #N to the number 12
- that the calculator does arithmetic from left to right
- that parentheses are used to change the order in which arithmetic is done
- that ?\ can be used to make random numbers of various sizes
- how to write a program that gives the answer to division problems
- how to tell the answering service to accept numbers for the turtle
- how to write a program that rolls gamemasters' dice
- how to match coins with the computer
- how to make the turtle wiggle, using ?\
- how to make the calculator and the turtle cooperate to make animated designs

9

GETTING CONTROL

Numbers can be used to control the action of the computer objects that populate the PILOT world. In this chapter you will learn:

- how to compare numbers
- how to use the results of number comparisons to control objects
- how to play a number guessing game with the computer
- how to make the computer count and keep totals
- how the computer keeps track of what's true and what's false
- a surprising fact about coin tossing
- how to make the turtle bounce
- how to make beautiful turtle tracks

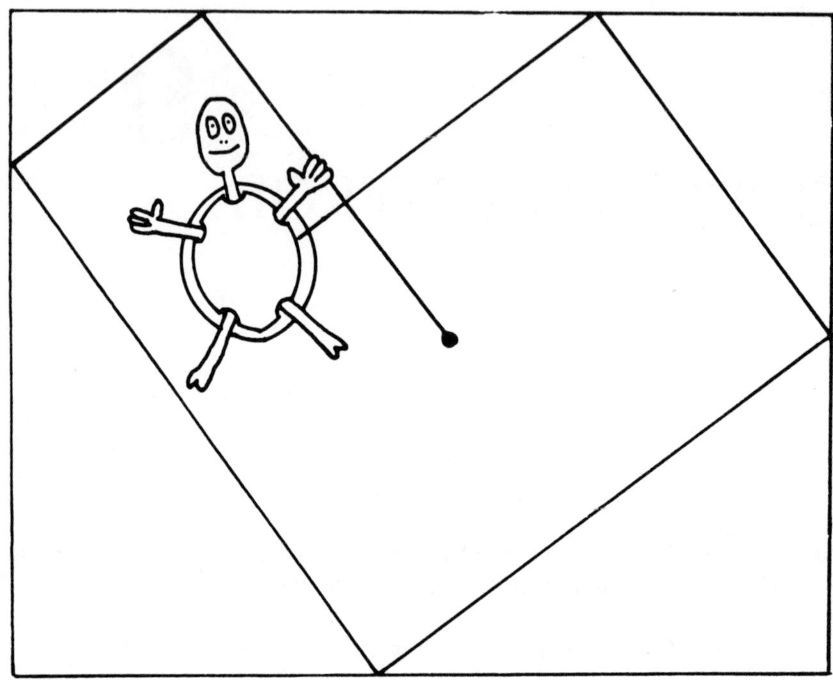

SMALLER < BIGGER

A flea is smaller than a tree. A goose is smaller than a caboose. A million is smaller than a trillion. One of the first things you learned about the world is that some things are smaller than others. We are going to talk a lot about LESS THAN in this chapter. You are going to learn how to control the turtle and the other computer objects using the sizes of numbers. It will save a lot of time if we have a quick way to say IS LESS THAN.

< MEANS "IS LESS THAN"

1<2 means 1 IS LESS THAN 2.
What does 3<5 mean?
Tell whether 2<5 is true or false.

ANSWERS: 3<5 means 3 IS LESS THAN 5. 2<5 is true.

The < looks a lot like a funnel. The smaller number goes at the small end of the funnel. The bigger number goes at the big end of the funnel.

How do you say that 0 is less than 100?
If 1>0 means 1 IS GREATER THAN 0, the 5>7 means what?
How do you say 4 is greater than 3?
If 7>8 true or false?
If 1<>2 means 1 IS NOT EQUAL TO 2, then what does 3<>5 mean?
How do you say 7 is not equal to 9?
Is 3<>3 true or false?

ANSWERS: 0<100; 5 IS GREATER THAN 7; 4>3; 7>8 is false; 3<>5 means 3 IS NOT EQUAL TO 5; 7<>9; 3<>3 is false.

In each of the following, put a 1 next to true statements, and a 0 next to false statements:

7<5   _________

2>1   _________

1<2   _________

2<>1   _________

2 = 1   _________

2<1   _________

(7/3 = 1)   _________

(7\3 = 1)   _________

COMPUTER LOGIC

The calculator knows the answer to questions like these. Try this:

```
C: #N = (5<6)
T: #N
```

You see this:

```
C: #N = (5<6)
T: #N
1
```

The calculator got the right answer.

What will these commands type on the screen?

```
C: #N = (5<2)
T: #N
```

The typer types 0, since (5<2) is false. We'll use this computer logic to make some games.

A LITTLE GUESSING GAME

Here is a program that uses the sizes of numbers to control the typer. The computer chooses a number between 0 and 3. Then, the computer asks you to guess the number. If your number equals the computer's number, then the typer types YOU GOT IT.

Try this program:

```
100 C: #A = ?\4          #A = 0, 1, 2, 3
110 *GUESS
120 , T:GUESS MY NUMBER
130 , A: #B               ACCEPT THE ANSWER #B
140 , T(#A=#B): YOU GOT IT     TYPE IF #A
                                    EQUALS #B
170 , J(#A<>#B): *GUESS        JUMP IF #A ISN'T
                                    EQUAL TO #B
RUN
```

When you RUN this program, you see this:

```
GUESS MY NUMBER
□
```

We typed 1 and saw this:

GUESS MY NUMBER
1
GUESS MY NUMBER
□

We typed 0 and saw this:

GUESS MY NUMBER
1
GUESS MY NUMBER
0
YOU GOT IT

READY
□

The typer and the jumper and all the other computer objects that you have met can be controlled by the sizes of numbers. For example:

T(#A = #B):

only types when #A equals #B.

J(#A <> #B):

only jumps when #A is not equal to #B.

When will T(0<1): type?
When will T(1<0): type?
When will T(#A = 3): type?

ANSWERS:

T(0<1): will always type, since 0<1 is true.
T(1<0): will never type, since 1<0 is never true.
T(#A=3): will type just when #A equals 3.

Fill in the space inside the parentheses so that the program will type BANG when #N is less than 5.

```
10 A: #N
20 T(     ): BANG
```

Fill in line 30 so that the program ends if #X is greater than 9.

```
10 *TOP
20 A:#X
30 ______
40 J:*TOP
```

ANSWERS: T(#N<5):; 30 E(#X>9):

A BETTER GAME

You can improve the last program and get a more interesting game. Lines 150 and 160 will give you helpful information about your guess. Line 100 will make the game a bit more challenging for you.

```
100 C: #A = ?\100         #A = 0, . . . ,99
110 *GUESS
120 , T: GUESS MY NUMBER
130 , A: #B
140 , T(#A=#B): YOU GOT IT        TYPE IF #A=#B
150 , T(#A<#B): TOO BIG           TYPE IF #A<#B
160 , T(#A>#B): TOO SMALL         TYPE IF #A>#B
170 , J(#A<>#B): *GUESS           JUMP IF #A<>#B
```

Here is what you see when you RUN the program:

```
GUESS MY NUMBER
▢
```

We tried the number 50. Here is what we saw:

```
GUESS MY NUMBER
50
TOO BIG
GUESS MY NUMBER
▢
```

We typed 20 and saw this:

```
GUESS MY NUMBER
50
TOO BIG
GUESS MY NUMBER
20
TOO SMALL
GUESS MY NUMBER
▢
```

Now you try it. Can you guess the number in six tries? Good luck.
Are you getting good at the game? Try a new version. Change line 100 to this:

```
100 C: #A = ?\1000
```

Now the random number is between 0 and 999. Can you guess the number in less than ten tries?

COUNTER POINT

The computer can keep track of the number of tries that you make. You can make the computer count by adding these lines to your program:

105 C: #N = 0 ☞ #N WILL KEEP COUNT
135 C: #N = #N + 1 ☞ INCREASE #N BY 1
165 T: #N TRIES ☞ TELL THE NUMBER OF TRIES

Now when you RUN the program, you see this:

```
GUESS MY NUMBER
□
```

If you type 50, then you see:

```
GUESS MY NUMBER
50
1 TRIES
□
```

The computer will count the number of tries that you make.
When you finally guess the number, you will see something like this:

```
YOU GOT IT
8 TRIES
READY
□
```

COUNT DOWN

Here is a change that will put the pressure on you. This change will give you just ten tries to guess the computer's number. The game will stop when your ten tries are all used up. Only lines 105, 135, 165, and 168 need to be added or changed. Here is the whole program written out for you to see:

```
100 C: #A = ?\1000
105 C: #N = 10
110 *GUESS
120 , T: GUESS MY NUMBER
130 , A: #B
135 , C: #N = #N − 1
140 , T(#A=#B): YOU GOT IT
150 , T(#A<#B): TOO BIG
160 , T(#A>#B): TOO SMALL
165 , T: #N TRIES LEFT
168 , E(#N=0):
170 , J(#A<>#B): *GUESS
```

Now, when you run this program you will see something like this after your first try:

```
GUESS MY NUMBER
20
TOO LOW
9 TRIES LEFT
GUESS MY NUMBER
□
```

SOMETHING ABOUT TRUTH

Remember that the computer keeps track of truth and falsity using 0's and 1's. The computer gives a value of 1 to true statements and a value of 0 to false statements.

What is the value of the statement $(2=1)$?

Your computer uses the value of statements to control the operation of commands. For example, the command

T(#X = 2): SOMETIMES

will only type when the statement (#X = 2) evaluates to 1. The command

T(1): TOO TOO TRUE

will always work. The number 1 turns on the command. The command

T(0): NO NO NEVER

will never type. The number 0 turns off the command.
What do you suppose the computer will do with other numbers?
   Try this command

T(2): WELL, WELL, WELL

Try this command

T(−1): NOPE

ANSWERS: (2 = 1) has the value 0. The number 2 turns on the command.
The number −1 turns the command off.

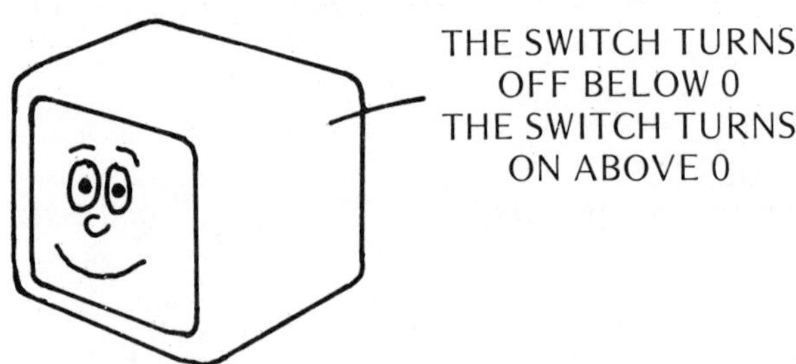

Here is a short program that will let you experiment to find out which numbers turn commands ON, and which numbers turn commands OFF.

10 *TOP
20 A: #N

30 T(#N): #N TURNS COMMANDS ON

```
40 T(−#N): #N TURNS COMMANDS OFF
50 J:TOP
```

Which of these numbers act like true statements?

    5, −1, 0, −0, −2, 100

Positive numbers turn commands ON. Negative numbers and 0 turn commands OFF.

If #N turns commands on, what does −#N do?

Can you find a number #N such that both #N and −#N turn commands OFF?

ANSWERS: If #N turns commands on, then −#N turns commands off; The number 0 is its own inverse −0=0. Both 0 and −0 turn commands off.

A VERY IMPORTANT NUMBER TO GUESS: Coins may be fair or unfair. If you flip a coin 100 times, you probably expect it to come up heads around half the time. That's about 50 heads. Here's the question: how many heads would it take before you would be almost certain that the coin was an unfair coin? Would you think the coin was unfair if it gave 51 heads? How about 60? What would surprise you? Write your answer here: _______

COIN TOSSER

The next program acts like a coin tosser. Up goes the coin, down comes heads or tails. Actually, computers like 0's and 1's better. The program tosses 100 coins and keeps track of the total number of 1's that appear.

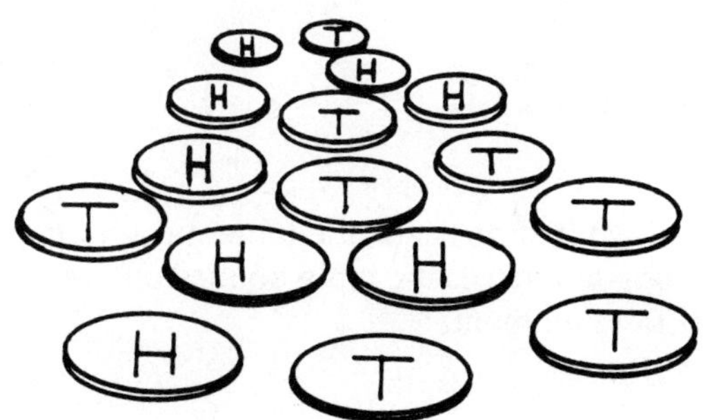

```
100 U:*INITIALIZER
110 *REPEAT
120 , U:*COINTOSSER
130 , U:*HEADCOUNTER
140 , U:*ENDPRINTER
150 , J:*REPEAT
200 *INITIALIZER
210 , C: #N = 100        THE TOSSES REMAINING
220 , C: #H = 0          THE NUMBER OF HEADS
230 , E:
300 *COINTOSSER
310 , C: #C = ?\2        #C = 0, OR 1
320 , C: #N = #N - 1     ONE TOSS DONE
330 , E:
400 *HEADCOUNTER
410 , C: #H = #H + #C     #C = 1 IS A HEAD
420 , E:
500 *ENDPRINTER
510 , E(#N):             RETURN WHILE #N IS POSITIVE
520 , T: #H HEADS
```

The surprising thing is this: The number of heads that occur in 100 tosses is almost never less than 35 or greater than 65. You must be very lucky or very unlucky to get other numbers.

VELOCITY TURTLE

You can use the calculator to make the turtle move in new and surprising ways. The next program makes the turtle bounce off the walls. Think about bouncing turtles for a moment.

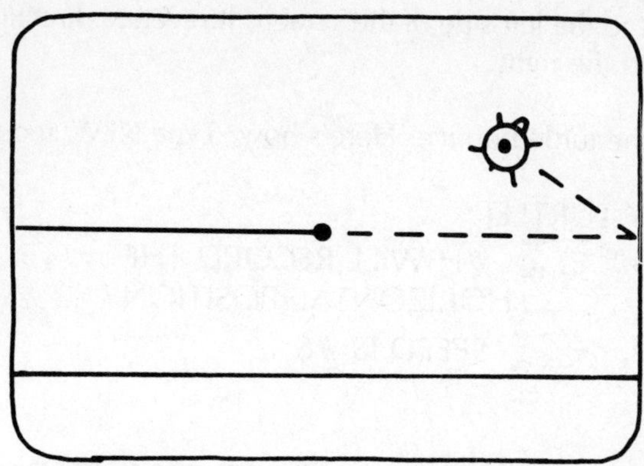

A turtle needs to start somewhere. Let's put our turtle in the center of the screen. Next, the turtle must be put into motion. Our turtle will march two turtle steps to the right each moment.

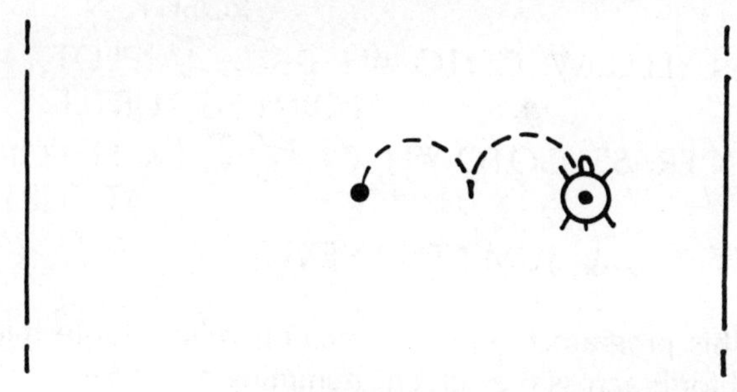

When the turtle get to the right edge, it must reverse its direction and march back toward the left.

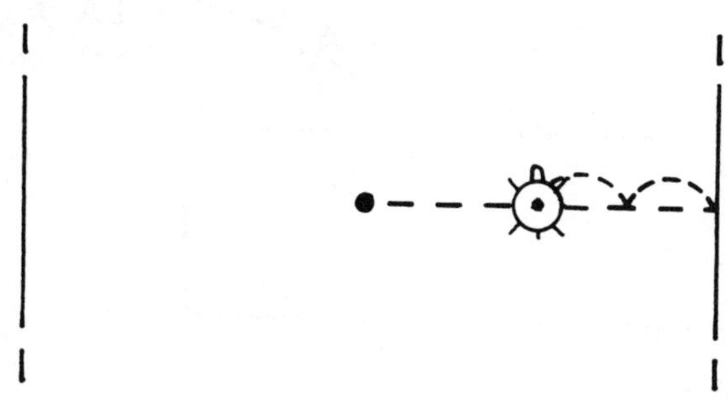

When the turtle gets to the left side of the screen, it reverses direction once more and marches to the right.

You can make the turtle bounce. Here's how. Type NEW and try this:

100 [VELOCITY TURTLE]
110 C:#H = 0   #H WILL RECORD THE
                        HORIZONTAL POSITION
140 C: #S = 2   SPEED IS #$
170 SO: #S
180 *NEXT
190 , C(#H>60): #S = −#S   REVERSE SPEED AT
                                    RIGHT WALL
200 , C(#H<−60): #S = −#S   REVERSE SPEED AT
                                    LEFT WALL
230 , C: #H = #H + #S   COMPUTE NEXT
                              POSITION
250 , GR: PEN YELLOW; GOTO #H, 0   PLOT
                              POINT AT TURTLE
260 , GR: PEN ERASE; GOTO #H, 0   ERASE POINT
                                    AT TURTLE
270 , J: *NEXT   JUMP TO *NEXT

When you RUN this program, you see a moving yellow turtle track that bounces back and forth across the screen, humming as it goes.

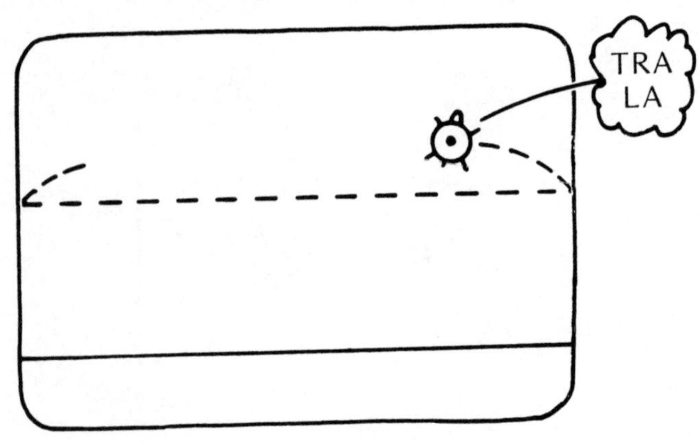

You can speed things up. Change line 120 to this:

    140 C: #S = 4

BOX TURTLE

Your turtle can do more exciting bounces. If you add a few lines to the last program, it will let the turtle bounce around the whole screen. Here is the whole program. The new lines are marked with ———▶. This program does a lot.

```
    100 [VELOCITY TURTLE]
    110 C: #H = 0        #H IS THE HORIZONTAL POSITION
➤   120 C: #V = 0        #V IS THE VERTICAL POSITION
➤   130 T: SPEED IN THE HORIZONTAL DIRECTION?
➤   140 A: #S           #S IS HORIZONTAL SPEED
➤   150 T: SPEED IN THE VERTICAL DIRECTION
➤   160 A:#T            #T IS VERTICAL SPEED
➤   170 SO: #S,#T
    180 *NEXT
    190 , C(#H>60): #S = − #S      REVERSE SPEED AT
                                       RIGHT WALL
    200 , C(#H< −60): #S = − #S    REVERSE SPEED AT
                                       LEFT WALL
➤   210 , C(#V<30): #T = − #T      REVERSE SPEED AT
                                       BOTTOM
➤   220 , C(#V> − 30): #T = − #T   REVERSE SPEED AT
                                       TOP
    230 , C: #H = #H + #S          COMPUTE NEXT
                                       POSITION
➤   240 , C: #V = #V + #T          COMPUTE NEXT
                                       POSITION
➤   250 , GR: PEN YELLOW; GOTO #H,#V    PLOT
                                   POINT AT TURTLE
➤   260 , GR: PEN ERASE; GOTO #H,#V     ERASE POINT
                                       AT TURTLE
    270 , J: *NEXT      JUMP TO *NEXT
```

When you run the previous program, you see this:

SPEED IN THE HORIZONTAL DIRECTION?
□

Type 1. You see this:

SPEED IN THE HORIZONTAL DIRECTION?
1
SPEED IN THE VERTICAL DIRECTION?
□

Type 2. You see this:

Run the program using the numbers 2 and 3 for the speeds.
Run the program using the numbers 2 and 4 for the speeds.
Experiment.

A BIG SURPRISE

Take away line 260, and the turtle will leave some beautiful tracks. Use 1 for horizontal speed, and 2 for vertical speed. You see something like this:

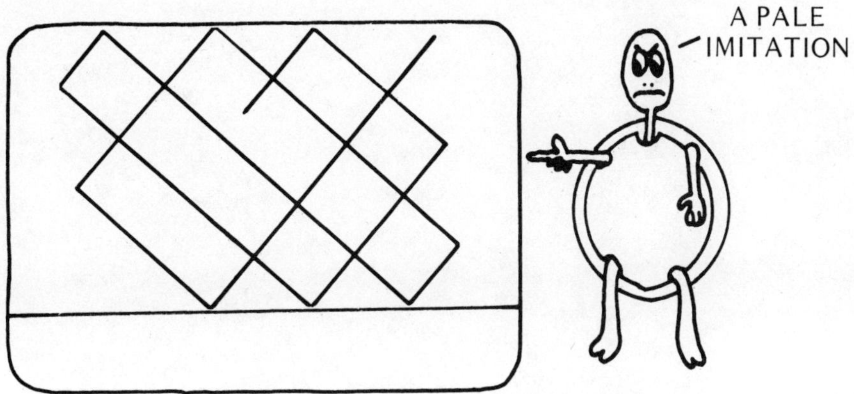

Use 3 and 5 for the speed numbers. You see this:

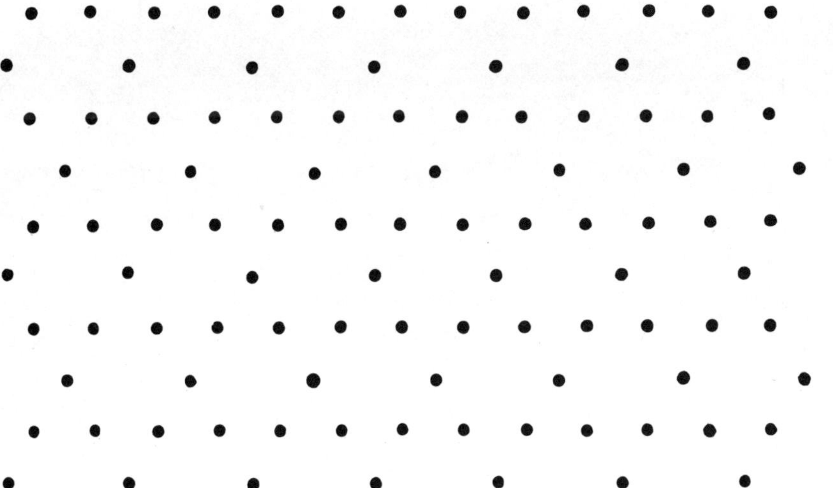

Try other small numbers. There are some beautiful designs to be seen.

ANOTHER SURPRISE

Change line 250 to this:

    250 GR: PEN YELLOW; DRAWTO #H,#V

SELF-TEST ON CHAPTER 9

1. Put a 1 next to the true statements, and a 0 next to the false statements.

   0<1   ______
   2<>2   ______
   5>1   ______
   (5\2=1)   ______

2. What will the following program type on the screen?

   ```
   10 A: #N = 1
   20 T(#N>1): ABBA
   30 T(#N=1): DABBA
   40 T(#N<1): DOO
   ```

   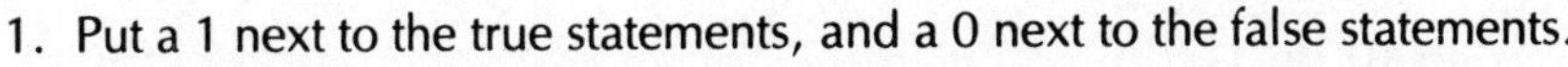

3. What will this program type?

   ```
   10 T(0): THIS
   20 T(1): THAT
   30 T(-1): THESE
   40 T(2): THOSE
   ```

4. What will this program type on the screen?

   ```
   10 #N = 0
   20 *TOP
   30 C: #N = #N + 1
   40 T: #N
   50 J:*TOP
   ```

____

____

5. Add a command at line 30 to make the program end when #A equals 5.

```
10 *TOP
20 A: #A
30 ______
40 J: *TOP
```

6. Add a command at line 30 to make the program jump to *TOP when #X is less than 10.

```
10 *TOP
20 A: #X
30 ______
```

7. Fill in the space between the parentheses in lines 30 and 40 so that when #R equals 0, the typer types TAILS, and when #R equals 1, the typer types HEADS.

```
10 *TOP
20 C: #R = ?\2
30 T(    ): HEADS
40 T(    ): TAILS
50 J: *TOP
```

8. Write a program that accepts numbers, and then types POSITIVE if the number is greater than 0, and NEGATIVE if the number is less than 0.

```
10 ______________
20 ______________
30 ______________
40 ______________
50 ______________
```

9. Add a command at lines 70 and 80 so that if #A equals the sum #S, then the typer will type YES, and if #A doesn't equal the sum #S, then the typer will type NO.

```
10 *TOP
20 C: #X = ?\10
30 C: #Y = ?\10
40 C: #S = #X + #Y
50 T: #X + #Y = ?
60 A: #A
70 ______
80 ______
90 J: *TOP
```

10. A coin is tossed 100 times and comes up heads exactly 70 times. Is that surprising or not?

ANSWERS:

1. 1, 0, 0, 1
2. The program will type DABBA.
3. The program will type THAT and THOSE.
4. The program is a counter and will type the numbers 1, 2, 3, . . . in a column on the screen.
5. 30 E(#A = 5):
6. 30 J(#X<10): *TOP
7. 30 T(#R = 1): HEADS

     40 T(#R = 0): TAILS

8. 10 *TOP

     20 A: #N
     30 T(#N>0): POSITIVE
     40 T(#N<0): NEGATIVE
     50 J: *TOP

9. 70 T(#A = #S): YES

     80 T(#A<>#S): NO

10. If a fair coin is tossed 100 times, the number of heads will nearly always be between 35 and 65. It very, very rarely will get to be 70.

SUMMARY OF CHAPTER 9

In this chapter you learned:

- that < means IS LESS THAN
- that > means IS GREATER THAN
- that <> means IS NOT EQUAL TO
- that the computer gives a value of 1 to true statements and a value of 0 to false statements
- that the truth or falsity of statements can control the operation of the PILOT computer objects
- that C: #N = #N + 1 makes a counter
- that C: #N = #N − 1 counts backwards
- how to make coin tosser that tosses 100 coins and counts the total number of heads
- that the number of heads that occur in 100 tosses of a fair coin will fall between 35 and 65 almost always
- how to make the turtle bounce off the walls

10

STRINGS AND THINGS

Words and letters are everywhere. The computer can help us deal with all the words and letters. In this chapter you will learn:

- how to associate messages so that one message can help recall another
- how the string function $ associates message strings
- how to make a computer directory that stores and recalls information for you
- that the Jump-on-Match command JM: works with the Match command M:
- that multiple matches and multiple jumps can be made
- how to write a streamlined version of turtle graphics language that is very simple to use
- how to write interactive stories that allow the reader to make choices that determine the next scene

THE STRING ASSOCIATION

When we say string, we mean a string of letters or other keyboard characters.

—I—AM—A—STRING—

Some strings are related to one another. For example, your name is a string, and so is your address. Your name and address are two strings which go together. Here are some other examples of associated strings:

times and appointments
names and birthdays
states and capitals
planets and facts about the planets
items and prices
places and distances
towns and populations
titles of songs and the musicians

Add a few examples of your own to the list.

All these pairs share something important in common. For each first string, there is only one second string that goes with it. The PILOT language was built to deal with just this situation.

THE STRING FUNCTION $

The PILOT language has an elegant way of associating one string with another string. The dollar sign ($) is the secret. When you put $ in front of any string, then the string is turned into the name of a place where a string is stored. You will store the associated string in that place. Here are some examples that show how this works:

We wish to associate CAT with BIRD. Type this:

A: $CAT = BIRD   [RETURN]

Now, to get the information about CAT, just tell the typer

T: $CAT   [RETURN]

The typer finds the information and types

BIRD

There is more to this story. Here is a question. You can probably guess the answer.

If $CAT = BIRD, and $BIRD = BUG, then what is $$CAT? _______
The answer is $$CAT = BUG. This is the clue to how the computer deals with the dollar sign, $.

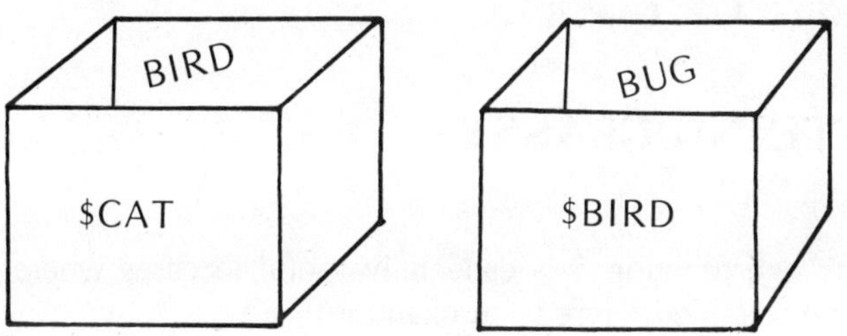

If $MORDRED = WIZARD, and $WIZARD = INTELLIGENCE16, then $$MORDRED = ?
The computer finds the first $ sign in $$MORDRED. The $ sign tells the computer that this is the name of the place where a string is stored. The computer finds the second $ sign. That tells the computer that it hasn't yet got the address. It must look at the location $MORDRED to get the address it needs. It goes to the address $MORDRED and finds the letters WIZARD stored there. Now the computer goes to the address $WIZARD and finds the string INTELLIGENCE16. The $ sign lead the computer on a treasure hunt.

The computer knows that a string that starts with $ is not a message, but an address.

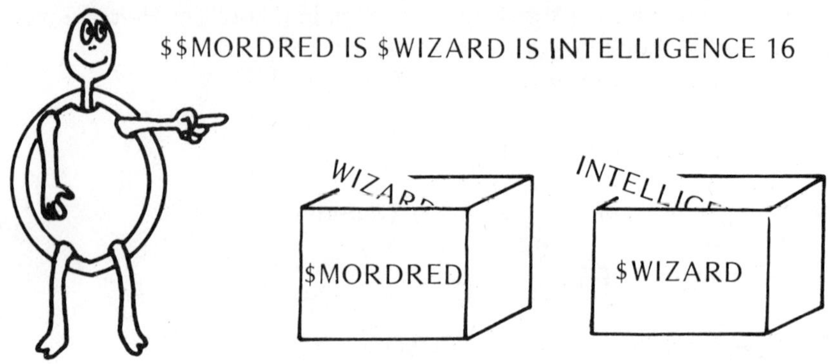

Here is an example to try:

```
10 A: $A = B
20 A: $B = C
30 A: $C = A
40 T: A, $A, $$A, $$$A, $$$$A
```

ANSWER: A, B, C, A, B

SOMETHING CLASSY

The dollar sign function $ is especially useful in cases where something needs to be classified. Here is an example:

```
JONES IS GRUMPY BUT NICE
SMITH IS SWEET AND SHY
BAKER IS CLEVER AND KIND
```

You can store this sort of information in your computer this way:

```
10 A: $JONES = GRUMPY BUT NICE
20 A: $SMITH = SWEET AND SHY
30 A: $BAKER = CLEVER AND KIND
```

Now that the information is stored, a simple program will get the information for you when you need it:

```
100 *NEXT
110 , T: NAME?
120 , A:$NAME
130 , T: $NAME IS $$NAME
140 , J:*NEXT
```

When you run this program, here is what you see:

NAME?

If you type in JONES, then the computer finds $JONES and prints this:

JONES IS GRUMPY BUT NICE

At line 120 the computer stops and the answering service accepts the name JONES when you type it.

120 A:$NAME

The string JONES is stored at the address $NAME.
At line 130 the typer is called by the command

130 T: $NAME IS $$NAME

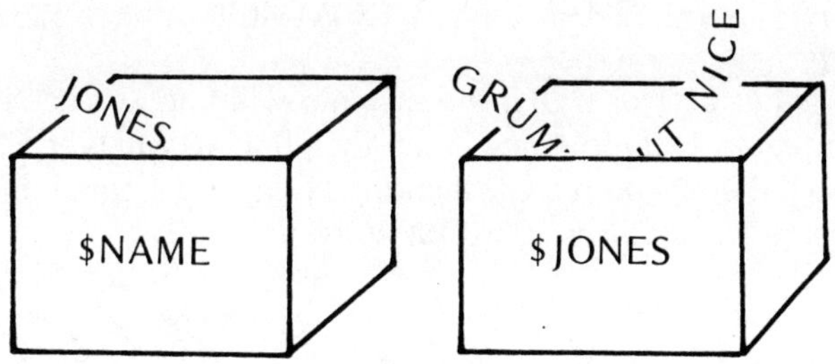

The typer goes to $NAME and finds the string JONES. The typer types

JONES IS

Next, the typer sees that it must go to the address $$NAME. The typer finds that $NAME contains the string JONES, so the address where the message is stored is $JONES. The typer goes to $JONES and finds the message GRUMPY BUT NICE. The typer completes its job and you see:

JONES IS GRUMPY BUT NICE

JUMP-ON-MATCH

Back in chapter VI you learned about the matcher. The matcher can match one or more strings against a message accepted by the answering service. Here is a program to remind you how the matcher works:

```
10 T: NAME A COMMON PET
20 A:
30 M: CAT, DOG
40 TY: YES, THAT'S COMMON
50 TN: NO, THAT'S NOT COMMON
```

If you type either CAT or DOG, the matcher will find a match and will set the Y flag equal to 1. If the Y flag is set, then line 40 will type YES, THAT'S COMMON. If there is no match, then the N flag is set equal to 1, and line 50 will type NO, THAT'S NOT COMMON.

There will be times when you will want to respond with more than a simple type command when the match is made. You will want to perform a whole program module in honor of the match. There is a way to make the computer jump to a labeled line when a match is made. The JUMP-ON-MATCH command JM: will do the deed.

Type NEW and try this example:

```
110 , T: DOG OR CAT?
120 , A:          ACCEPT ANSWER
130 , M: DOG, CAT          MATCH FOR THESE WORDS
140 , JM: *DOG, *CAT          JUMP TO THESE
150 , E:

200 *DOG
210 , T:WOOF WOOF
220 , E:

300 *CAT
310 , T: MEOW MEOW
320 , E:
```

Here's what you see when you run this program:

```
DOG OR CAT?
□
```

Type DOG and press RETURN . You see:

```
DOG OR CAT?
DOG
WOOF WOOF

READY
□
```

The answering service accepted your answer DOG. The matcher checked you answer to see if it matched DOG or CAT. DOG matched your answer. The matcher set the Y flag to 1, and also furnished information to the jumper that the first word matched. The jumper then went to the first line mentioned *DOG. At *DOG the typer typed WOOF WOOF.

A DIRECTORY

Here is a program that stores and recalls pairs of strings. When you run this program, it asks whether you want to store or recall a pair. This program has lots of uses. You can store names and telephone numbers, times and appointments, or any other pairs that are important to you. Type NEW and give it a try.

```
100 *DIRECTORY
110 , T: STORE OR RECALL?
120 , A:
130 , M: S, STORE, R, RECALL          MATCH FOR THESE
140 , JM: *STORE, *STORE, *RECALL, *RECALL          JUMP
150 , J: *DIRECTORY          JUMP TO *DIRECTORY

200 *STORE
210 , T: FIRST STRING?
220 , A: $FIRST          ACCEPT A STRING NAMED $FIRST
230 , T: SECOND STRING?
240 , A: $$FIRST          $$FIRST IS ASSOCIATED WITH
                                              $FIRST
250 , J: *DIRECTORY

300 *RECALL
310 , T: FIRST STRING?
320 , A: $FIRST          ACCEPT A STRING NAMED $FIRST
330 , T: $$FIRST          $$FIRST IS ASSOCIATED WITH
                                              $FIRST
340 , J: *DIRECTORY
```

Here is what you see when you RUN the program:

```
STORE OR RECALL?
☐
```

Type S RETURN . The computer jumps to *STORE. You see:

```
STORE OR RECALL?
S
FIRST STRING?
☐
```

Type COLUMBUS RETURN . The computer stores COLUMBUS under
the name $FIRST. You see:

```
STORE OR RECALL?
S
FIRST STRING?
COLUMBUS
SECOND STRING?
☐
```

Type 1492 RETURN . The computer stores 1492 under the name $$FIRST
which is the same as $COLUMBUS. You see:

```
STORE OR RECALL?
S
FIRST STRING?
COLUMBUS
SECOND STRING?
1492
STORE OR RECALL
☐
```

You can now store more pairs of strings, or recall some pair that is stored.
Let's see if the information can be recalled.

Type R RETURN . The computer jumps to *RECALL. You see this:

```
STORE OR RECALL?
R
FIRST STRING?
□
```

Type COLUMBUS RETURN . The computer stores COLUMBUS under
the name $FIRST. Then the computer types $$FIRST. $$FIRST is the same
as COLUMBUS. $COLUMBUS is an address that contains the string 1492.
You see:

```
STORE OR RECALL?
R
FIRST STRING?
COLUMBUS
1492
STORE OR RECALL?
□
```

The computer jumped to *DIRECTORY. You can store or recall a pair.

Store this list so that you can recall items by their number:

```
1 CALL MO
2 PICK UP MO
3 ASK FLO
```

Type S RETURN   to start storing. When the computer asks for FIRST
STRING?, you type in 1. When the computer asks for SECOND STRING?,
you type in CALL MO. Continue to STORE until the whole list is entered.
   Now recall an item from the list. When the computer asks
STORE OR RECALL?, you type R RETURN . When the computer asks
for the FIRST STRING?, you type a number. Type 3 RETURN . The
computer types ASK FLO.

Store this list so that you can recall items by color:

    RED ACTIVE
    YELLOW ATTENTIVE
    BLUE PASSIVE

DUMP

There is a quick way to look at all the strings you have stored. Type this:

    DUMP   [RETURN]

The computer dumps all the string names and all the strings onto the screen for you to see. You see something like this:

    $COLUMBUS = '1492'
    $1 = 'CALL MO'
    $2 = 'PICK UP MO'
    $RED = 'ACTIVE'
    $YELLOW = 'ATTENTIVE'
    $BLUE = 'PASSIVE'

This can be useful if you forget what you've got stored.

SAVING PROGRAMS

If you have a cassette player or a disk drive, then you might like to save your program and data. Read Appendix A at the back of the book to learn how to SAVE and LOAD your programs.

TURTLE TRACK

You can use the powerful Jump-on-Match command to write a simpler, more streamlined version of turtle graphics. This version is even suitable for small children. It uses single letter commands that are easy to type. The four commands are:

    F FORWARD
    B BACKWARD
    R RIGHT 30 DEGREES
    L LEFT 30 DEGREES

The program allows you to type one of the letters F, B, R, or L followed by RETURN . The turtle will immediately follow your command. For example, the following list of commands will draw the line shown.

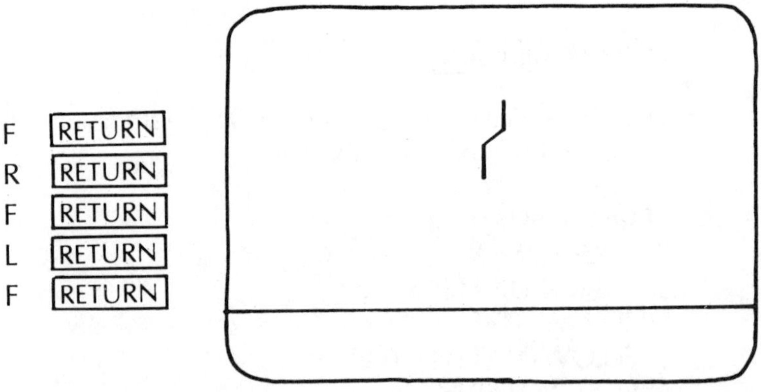

Here is what the program will do. First, the computer will stop and let you type in a letter. When you type a letter and press RETURN , the computer will match your letter against the list of command letters. If a match is found, then the computer will jump to a labeled module that does the task. When the task is complete, the computer will jump to the top of the program and let you type in another letter.

Here is the streamlined turtle program:

100 *TOP
110 , A: ACCEPT A COMMAND LETTER
120 , M; F, B, R, L MATCH FOR THE COMMAND
                                    LETTER
130 , JM: *F, *B, *R, *L JUMP TO THE RIGHT
                                    PLACE
140 , J: *TOP JUMP TO TOP IF NO MATCH

```
200 *F
210 , GR: DRAW 5
220 , J: *TOP

300 *B
310 , GR: DRAW −5
320 , J: *TOP

400 *R
410 , GR: TURN 30
420 , J: *TOP

500 *L
510 , GR: TURN −30
520 , J: *TOP
```

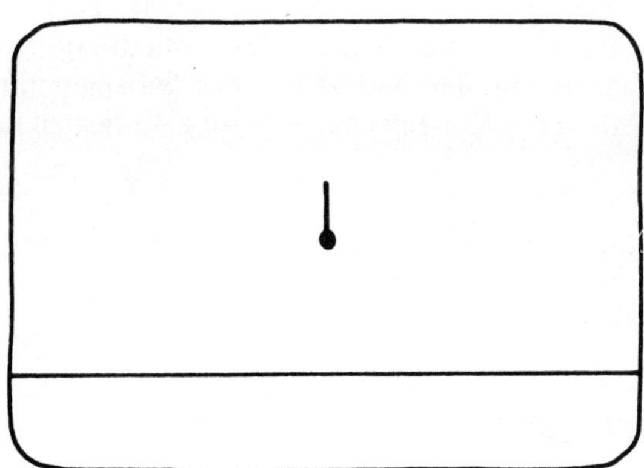

DRAW FORWARDS

DRAW BACKWARDS

TURN RIGHT

TURN LEFT

When you RUN the program, you first see a blank screen. Type F
[RETURN] . You see this:

Press   [SYSTEM RESET] . Make a hexagon like this:

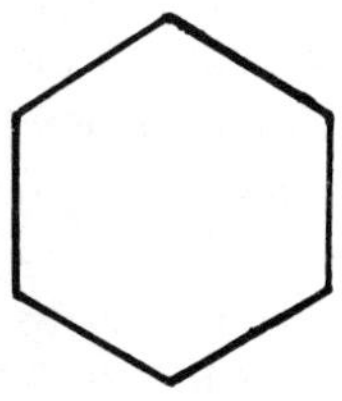

Press SYSTEM RESET . Make a triangle like this:

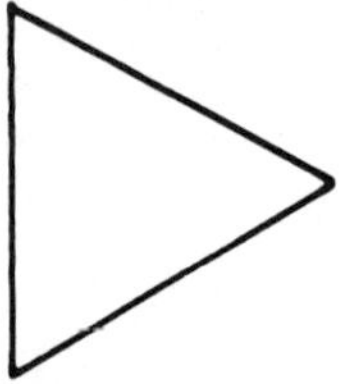

Experiment.

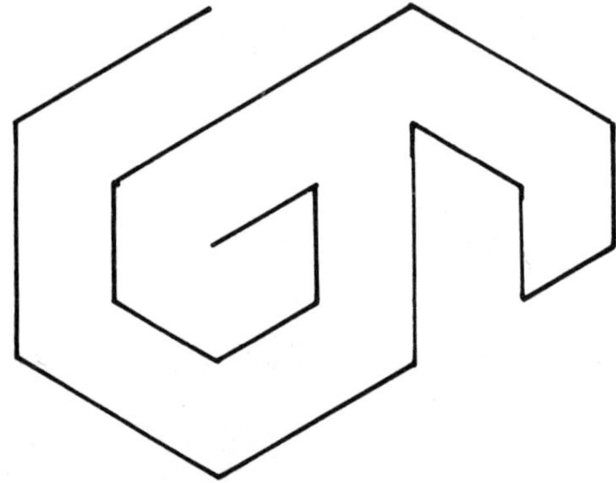

Did you notice that you can't make a 45-degree turn with this program? There is an easy cure. Change lines 410 and 510 so that the angle turned is 15 degrees, instead of 30. Three 15-degree turns make a 45-degree turn.

    410 , GR: TURN 15
    510 , GR: TURN −15

Now you have more control.

INTERACTIVE STORY

The techniques that work so well for the turtle can also be used to write interactive stories. An interactive story is one in which the reader gets to make decisions about the way the story develops. When you run the story program, a scene is set:

    YOU ARE IN A LARGE AND DIMLY LIT ROOM.
    AT THE FAR END OF THE ROOM IS A DOORWAY.

IN THE CENTER OF THE ROOM IS A SPIRAL STAIRCASE
THAT WINDS UP THROUGH A HOLE IN THE CEILING.
WHICH WAY DO YOU WANT TO GO?
DOOR
STAIRS

Now you get to make a choice. The next scene that is presented to you
depends on the choice you make. If you choose DOOR, then the next scene
will be in the hall. If you choose the STAIRS, then the next scene will be
on the stairs. Each of those scenes will give you choices, and the choices
will take you to new scenes and to new adventures.

It is easy to write interactive stories in PILOT. The PILOT language was
designed for just such tasks. The fun and excitement of computer-aided
stories and adventures is that others can enjoy the worlds that your imagination creates. More than one person can work on an adventure story.
When two or more people develop a story, there are surprises for everybody.

Here is the program that controls the first scene of our story:

```
100 [INTERACTIVE STORY]
150 *ROOM1
```

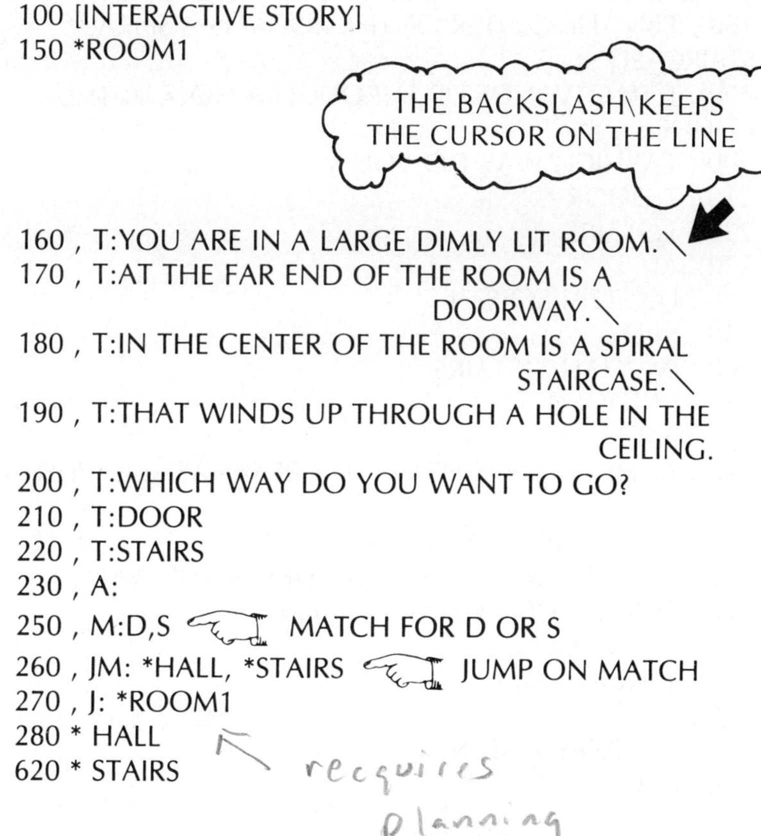


```
160 , T:YOU ARE IN A LARGE DIMLY LIT ROOM.\
170 , T:AT THE FAR END OF THE ROOM IS A
                        DOORWAY.\
180 , T:IN THE CENTER OF THE ROOM IS A SPIRAL
                        STAIRCASE.\
190 , T:THAT WINDS UP THROUGH A HOLE IN THE
                        CEILING.
200 , T:WHICH WAY DO YOU WANT TO GO?
210 , T:DOOR
220 , T:STAIRS
230 , A:
250 , M:D,S
260 , JM: *HALL, *STAIRS
270 , J: *ROOM1
280 * HALL
620 * STAIRS
```

When you RUN this program, you will find that it ends as soon as you make a choice. There is no scene at line *HALL and *STAIRS. What does that hall look like? Where do those stairs go? You can use you own imagination to create new rooms, tunnels, dragons and treasures. Our program follows. You can use it to see how to hook scenes together. Notice the module to clear the screen at line 120. That turns out to be useful. Have fun.

```
100 [INTERACTIVE STORY]
110 J:*ROOM1
120 *CLEARSCREEN
130 , T:  [ESC]   [SHIFT]     [CLEAR]
140 , E:
150 *ROOM1
160 , T:YOU ARE IN A LARGE DIMLY LIT ROOM. \
170 , T:AT THE FAR END OF THE ROOM IS DOORWAY. \
180 , T:IN THE CENTER OF THE ROOM IS A SPIRAL
STAIRCASE \
190 , T:THAT WINDS UP THROUGH A HOLE IN THE
CEILING.
200 , T:WHICH WAY DO YOU WANT TO GO?
210 , T:DOOR
220 , T:STAIRS
230 , A:
240 , U:*CLEARSCREEN
250 , M:D,S
260 , JM:*HALL, *STAIRS
270 , J:*ROOM1
280 *HALL
290 , T:THE DOOR IS HEAVY. IT CREAKS AS YOU PUSH IT
OPEN. \
300 , T:AS IT OPENS YOU SEE A STONE CORRIDOR. \
310 , T:CANDLES FLICKER IN NICHES IN THE WALL.
320 , T:WHAT DO YOU WANT TO DO?
330 , T:GO AHEAD
340 , T:TURN BACK
350 , A:
360 , U:*CLEARSCREEN
370 , M:G,T
```

380 , JM:*HALLUP, *ROOM1
390 , J:*HALL
400 *HALLUP
410 , T:THE CORRIDOR SLOPES STEEPLY UPWARD AND CURVES TO THE RIGHT. \
420 , T:YOU KEEP CLIMBING UNTIL YOU REACH A DOOR. \
430 , T:YOU TOUCH THE DOOR AND IT MOVES EASILY.
440 , T:WHAT DO YOU WANT TO DO?
450 , T:GO AHEAD
460 , T:TURN BACK
470 , A:
480 , U:*CLEARSCREEN
490 , M:G,T
500 , JM:*ROOM2, *HALLDOWN
510 , J:*HALLUP
520 *STAIRS
530 , T:THE BLACK, METAL STAIRCASE WOBBLES AS YOU CLIMB. \
540 , T:UP AND UP YOU CLIMB. YOU NEAR THE DARK HOLE IN THE CEILING.
550 , T:WHAT DO YOU WANT TO DO?
560 , T:GO AHEAD
570 , T:TURN BACK
580 , A:
590 , U:*CLEARSCREEN
600 , M:G,T
610 , JM:*ROOM2, *ROOM1
620 , J:*STAIRS
630 *ROOM2
640 , T:YOU ARE IN A BRIGHTLY LIT ROOM. THE SUN STREAMS \
650 , T:THROUGH WINDOWS IN THE ROOF HIGH ABOVE. \
660 , T:THE ROOMS IS FILLED WITH PILLOWS ON A SOFT RUG. \
670 , T:THERE IS A DOOR IN THE NORTH WALL, AND A STAIRWAY \
680 , T:SPIRALS DOWN THROUGH A HOLE IN THE FLOOR.

690 , T:WHAT DO YOU WISH TO DO?
700 , T:OPEN DOOR
710 , T:USE STAIRS
720 , T:STAY HERE
730 , A:
740 , U:*CLEARSCREEN
750 , M:O,U, S
760 , JM:*HALLDOWN, *STAIRDOWN, *END
770 , J:*ROOM2
780 *HALLDOWN
790 , T:THE DOOR OPENS EASILY. YOU SEE BEFORE YOU A CORRIDOR \
800 , T:LIGHTED BY CANDLES. IT SLOPES STEEPLY DOWNWARD. \
810 , T:YOU MUST WALK CAREFULLY TO AVOID SLIPPING. \
820 , T:AT LAST YOU SEE BEFORE YOU A LARGE WOODEN DOOR.
830 , T:WHAT DO YOU WISH TO DO?
840 , T:OPEN DOOR
850 , T:TURN BACK
860 A:
870 R:*CLEARSCREEN
880 , M:O,T
890 , JM:*ROOM1, *HALLUP
900 J:*HALLDOWN
910 *STAIRDOWN
920 , T:THE STAIRS SPIRAL DOWNWARD. YOU CLIMB CAREFULLY DOWN \
930 , T:THE RICKETY METAL STAIRS. \
940 , T:WHEN YOU REACH THE BOTTOM YOU TAKE A FEW STEPS AND LOOK ABOUT.
950 , J:*ROOM1
960 *END
970 , T:USE YOUR OWN IMAGINATION NOW. \
980 , T:CREATE WHAT YOU WISH.
990 , E:

Now you are on your own. A map may help. Create your own world.

SELF-TEST ON CHAPTER 10

1. If $NAME = BERT and $ERNIE = NAME, then $$ERNIE = ?

   ____

2. Tell what this program will type:

   ```
   10 A: $NUMBER = ONE
   20 A: $ONE = 1
   30 T: $$NUMBER
   ```

3. Add a command at line 40 so that this program will give the food that the animal eats.

   ```
   10 *TOP
   20 T: BIRD OR CAT?
   30 M: BIRD, CAT
   40 ______
   50 *B
   60 T: WORMS
   70 E:
   80 *C
   90 T: MILK
   ```

4. Add a command at line 35 so that the program will repeat the question BIRD or CAT? if you type anything but BIRD or CAT.

Problems 5–8 will refer to this next program:

```
100 *TOP
110 A:
120 M: A,B
130 JM: *A, *B
140 J: *TOP
150 *A
160 T: ALPHA
170 E:
180 *B
190 T: BETA
```

5. What will the above program type if you run it and then enter the letter A? _______

6. What will happen if you run the program and enter the letter C?

    ____

7. Change the program so that it will end if anything other than A or B is entered. Show your changed line below:

    ____

8. Change line 130 so that the program will type ALPHA if Z is entered.

    130 _______

9. What does the command DUMP do?

    ____

10. What will this program type?

```
10 T: KNURLY\
20 T: KNOBS
```

____

ANSWERS:

1. $$ERNIE = $NAME = BERT

2. The program types the number 1.

3.   40 JM: *B, *C

4.   35 JN: *TOP

5. If you type A, the program finds a match at line 120. Then, line 130 causes a jump to line *A. The typer types ALPHA.

6. If you enter C, no match is found at line 120. Line 130 will have no effect. Line 140 causes a jump to *TOP. The program waits to accept a message.

7. Change line 140 to E:

8. Change the match command on line 130 to M: D, B

9. The DUMP command shows you all the strings stored in the computer's memory.

10. KNURLYKNOBS. The backslash \ at the end of a type line causes the cursor to remain on that line instead of going to the beginning of the next line.

SUMMARY OF CHAPTER 10

In this chapter you learned:

- that the string function $ can be used to associate strings
- that a string preceded by $ is an address where a string may be stored
- that the jump-on-match command JM: works with the match command M:
- that you can make multiple matches and multiple jumps
- how to make a directory that stores and recalls associated strings
- that the DUMP command allows you to see all the strings that are stored in computer memory
- how to write a streamlined version of turtle graphics
- how to write interactive stories that allow the reader to make choices that determine the direction of the story

THE JOY OF JOYSTICKS

11

A joystick adds even more fun to ATARI* PILOT Language. You can play games with numbers, sounds, and graphics using your joystick. In this appendix you will learn:

- that the red trigger button on the joystick sends 0's and 1's to the computer

- how to use the trigger button to control sound and movement on the screen

- that the joystick sends numbers to the computer

- how to use the joystick numbers in your programs

- how to use the joysticks to control the turtle on the screen

THE JOY OF JOYSTICKS

Your ATARI* computer has four places on the front edge where you can plug in your joystick. In this section you will learn how to use the joystick to send numbers to the computer.

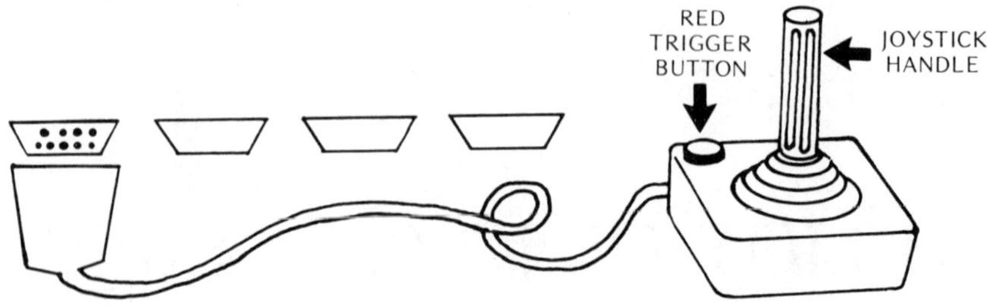

THE TRIGGER

See that red button on the base of the joystick? That's called the trigger. The trigger sends messages to the computer. You can see the trigger work. Plug the joystick into the first slot on the left. Type NEW and try this little program:

```
10 *TOP
20 T: %T8 [%T8 IS THE NUMBER SENT BY THE TRIGGER]
30 J:*TOP
RUN
```

You see this:

<pre>
0)
0 } ☞ TRIGGER NOT PRESSED
0)

1)
1 } ☞ TRIGGER PRESSED
1)
</pre>

The trigger sends the number 0 to the computer when it is not pressed. The trigger sends the number 1 when it is pressed. The number is stored in the computer under the special name %T8.

You can use the number sent by the trigger to control sounds. Type NEW and try this program:

```
10 C: #N = 0 [#N WILL BE THE SOUND NUMBER]
20 SO: #N [SOUND #N IS NOW ON]
```

```
30 *TOP
40 [IF THE TRIGGER EQUALS 1, INCREASE #N]
50 , C(%T8 = 1): #N = #N + 2
60 , J:*TOP [GO DO IT AGAIN]
RUN
```

Each time you press the trigger, the sound number #N is changed. When
#N is changed, the sound immediately changes.
   Add these two lines:

```
42 C: #N = #N - 1
44 PA:20
```

Now what happens when you RUN the program?
   Add this mysterious line:

```
46 C: @B712 = #N
```


FAST GAME

How are your reflexes today? Are you feeling fast? Here's a game that will
exercise your trigger finger. You need to be quick. When the computer
prints NOW, you must press the trigger button as fast as you can. The
computer will time your response. Give it a try.

```
110 *TOP
120 , C: #P = ?\60 + 60 [#P IS BETWEEN 60 and 120]
130 , PA:#P [PAUSE 1 TO 2 SECONDS]
160 , T: NOW!
170 , C: #T = 0 [START THE TIMER]
180 *TIMER
190 , C: #T = #T + 1 [INCREASE THE TIME COUNTER]
200 , J(%T8=0): *TIMER [JUMP IF NO TRIGGER]
210 , T:YOUR TIME IS #T
240 , T: READY?
250 , A: [WAIT FOR A RESPONSE]
260 , *TOP
```

Press the button as soon as the word NOW! appears. How fast can you do it?

Add these lines to make the computer keep track of your best time.

```
100 C: #B = 10000 [#B IS THE BEST SO FAR]
220 , T(#T<#B): THIS IS A NEW RECORD [CHECK IF #T IS
LESS THEN #B]
230 , C(#T<#B): #B = #T [IF NEW RECORD, BEST IS #T]
RUN
```

Did you notice that you can cheat at this game? If you hold down the button, you always win. That can be fixed.

```
140 , T(%T8 = 1): WAIT FOR THE SIGNAL
150 , J(%T8 = 1): *TOP          [JUMP IF TRIGGER IS EARLY]
```

Add a command at line 235 to play a sound when a record is set.
Add these lines to make the word NOW! appear at different places on the screen

```
152 , T:(ESC)(SHIFT)(CLEAR)          [THIS CLEARS THE
                                          SCREEN]
154 , C: #C = ?\35 [RANDOM COLUMN NUMBER]
156 , C: #L = ?\23 [RANDOM LINE NUMBER]
158 , POS: #C, #L [POSITION CURSOR]
```

```
YOUR TIME IS 16
THIS IS A NEW RECORD
```

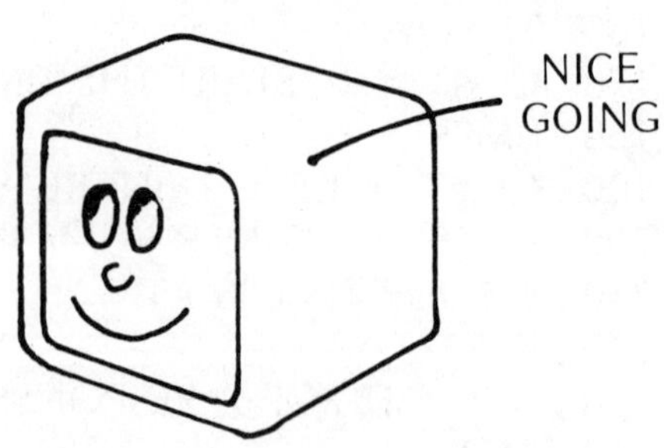

Here is short program that uses the trigger button. It does a lot. Give it a try:

```
100 C: #A = 0
110 *TOP
120 C(%T8 = 0): #A  =  - 30
130 C(%T8 = 1): #A  =  30
140 GR: GO 5; TURN #A
150 PA: 30
160 J:*TOP
RUN
```

Change line 140 to this:

```
140 GR: DRAW 5; TURN #A
```

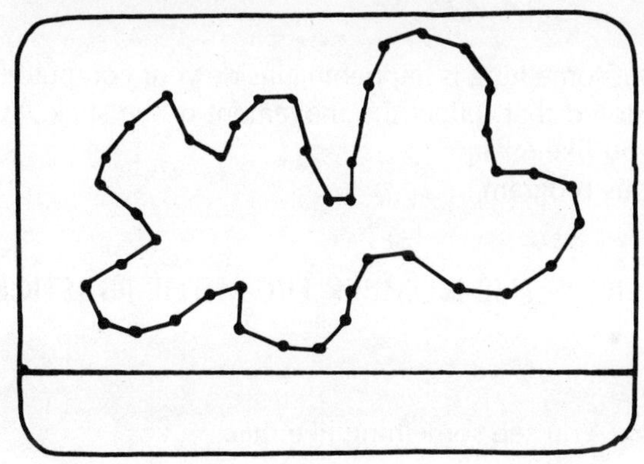

Now speed things up. Change line 150 to this:

```
150 PA: 10
```

How about a little sound?

```
105 SO: #A
```

This change makes a big difference:

```
120 C(%T8 = 0): #A  =  - 90
130 C(%T8 = 1): #A  =  90
```

Now you're on your own. Have fun.

THE JOYSTICK

Plug your joystick into the slot on the left. Move the stick. Do you see anything?

Nope, not a thing. But something is happening inside your computer. Some numbers are being stored that reflect the movement of the stick. You can see the numbers if you like.

Type NEW and try this program:

```
10 *TOP
20 T: %JO [ %JO IS THE NUMBER FROM THE JOYSTICK]
30 J: *TOP
RUN
```

Move the joystick. You see something like this:

Each joystick position sends a different number to the computer. Here is a picture of the nine stick positions and the numbers that go with them.

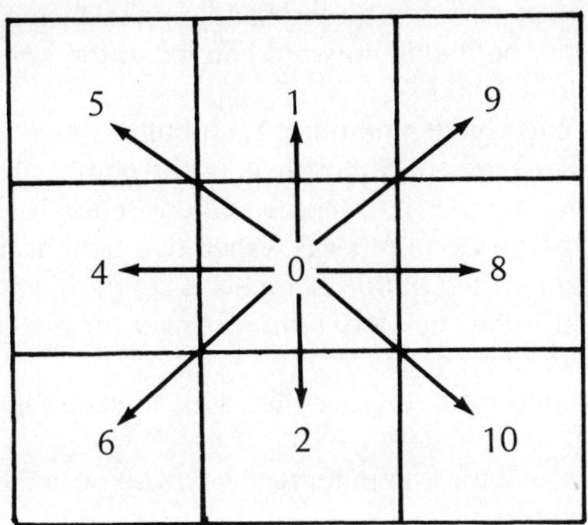

JOYSTICK FINGERS

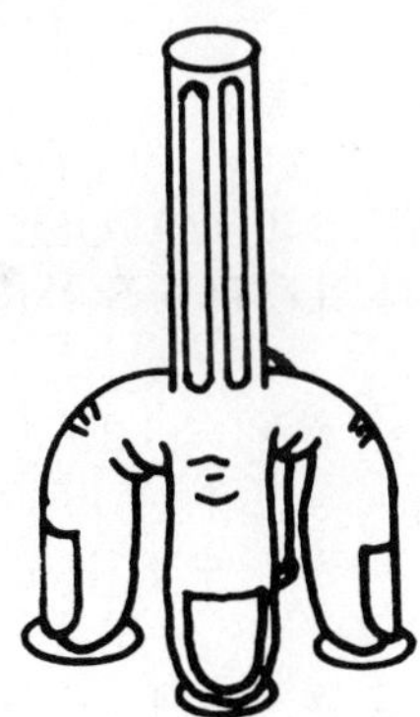

The joystick handle is connected to four fingers inside the base of the joystick. The four fingers rest lightly on four numbered buttons. The buttons look like this:

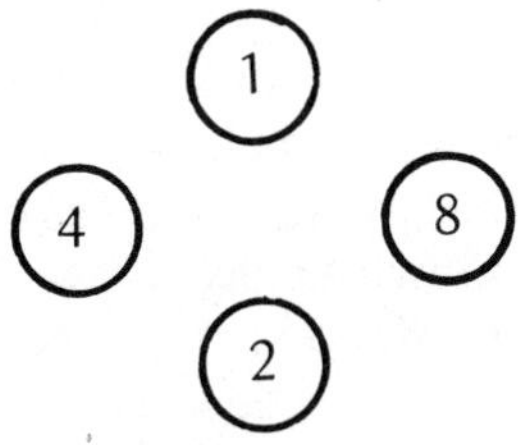

When you tilt the handle, the fingers press on the buttons. If you move the handle forward, then one finger presses button 1. If you pull the handle back, then one finger presses button 2. If you tilt the handle left, then one finger presses button 4. If you tilt the handle right, then one finger presses button 8. If you tilt the handle forward and left at the same time, then two fingers press buttons 1 and 4.

The buttons each have a number. Each button sends its number to the computer when it is pressed. Button 1 sends the number 1 to the computer. Button 2 sends the number 2 to the computer. Button 4 sends the number 4, and button 8 sends the number 8. When two buttons are pushed at the same time, the sum of the button numbers is sent to the computer.

When you push the stick forward, the finger presses button 1, and the number 1 is sent to the computer.

In what direction must you push the stick to send the number 9 to the computer?

What number will the computer receive if you push the stick to the left? What button is pressed?

ANSWERS: Up and right; 4

Here is a short program that uses the joystick number to control two sounds.

```
100 [STICKSOUNDS]
110 , C: #A = 0 [STARTING VALUE OF FIRST SOUND]
120 , C: #B = 0 [STARTING VALUE OF SECOND SOUND]
130 , SO: #A, #B [ENABLE THE SOUNDS]
140 *CHECKSTICK
150 , C(%JO=4): #A = #A − 1 [IF LEFT, DECREASE #A]
160 , C(%JO=8): #A = #A + 1 [IF RIGHT, INCREASE #A]
170 , C(%JO=2): #B = #B − 1 [IF BACKWARDS,
DECREASE #B]
180 , C(%JO=1): #B = #B + 1 [IF FORWARDS, INCREASE
#B]
190 , GR: DRAWTO #A, #B
200 , J:*CHECKSTICK
```

The joystick numbers can be easy to use. What you really want to know is whether the handle is tilted left or right, and whether the handle is pushed forward or pulled back. The joystick numbers hide that information. The program module *STICK, shown below, gives you just what you need. It computes a pair of numbers, #H and #K, at each position of the joystick. The number #H equals −1, 0, or 1 depending on whether the joystick tilts left, stays in the middle, or tilts right. The number #K equals −1, 0, or 1 depending on whether the joystick tilts forward, stays in the middle, or tilts back.

10 *TOP
20 , U: *STICK
30 , T: #H #K
40 , J: *TOP

100 *STICK
110 , C: #H = $-(\%J\emptyset/4 = 1) + (\%J\emptyset/4 = 2)$
120 , C: #K = $(\%J\emptyset\backslash4 = 1) - (\%J\emptyset\backslash4 = 2)$
130 , E:

The pairs #H, #K correspond to these positions:

-1,1	0,1	1,1
-1,0	0,0	0,1
-1,-1	0,-1	1,-1

You can use the joystick to draw on the screen. Change lines 30, 40, and 50 to get this:

10 *TOP
20 , U: *STICK
30 , C: #X = %X + #H [COMPUTE NEW X-COORDINATE]

40 , C: #Y = %Y + #K [COMPUTE NEW Y-COORDINATE]
50 , GR: GOTO #X, #Y [GOTO THE NEW POSITION]
60 , J: *TOP

Now RUN the program. What happens?
You see this:

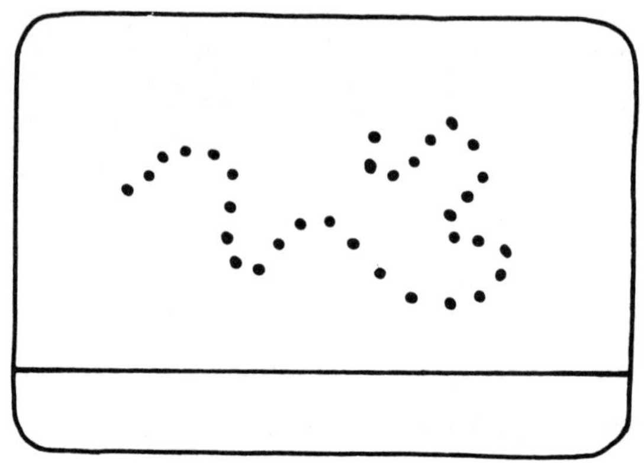

The dot moves in the direction you move the joystick.
See what happens when you change line 50 to this:

50 , GR: DRAWTO #X,#Y

What happens when you change line 50 to this:

50 , GR: DRAW #X,#Y

Try this:

50 , SO: #X,#Y

Now that you are expert at controlling the turtle's position, you are ready for something a shade more exciting. The next most exciting thing after position is velocity. Are you ready to speed? Here is a program that controls the speed and direction of the turtle. You'll have to be quick. Type NEW and give this a try:

100 *BEGIN
110 , C: #V = 0 [INITIAL VELOCITY IN X DIRECTION]
120 , C: #W = 0 [INITIAL VELOCITY IN Y DIRECTION]
130 *TOP
140 , GR: CLEAR [CLEAR THE SCREEN]
150 , U: *STICK [READ #H and #K FROM STICK MODULE]
160 , C: #V = #V + #H [CHANGE VELOCITY IN X
DIRECTION]
170 , C: #W = #W + #K [CHANGE VELOCITY IN Y
DIRECTION]
180 , C: #X = #X + #V [USE VELOCITY TO CHANGE
POSITION]
190 , C: #Y = #Y + #W [USE VELOCITY TO CHANGE
POSITION]
200 , GR: GOTO #X, #Y [MOVE TURTLE TO NEW
POSITION]
210 , U: *HEX [USE HEX MODULE TO DRAW TURTLE]
220 , T:#X #Y [JUST IN CASE TURTLE GETS LOST]
230 , J: *TOP [GO DO IT AGAIN]
240 *STICK [DECODE STICK MOVEMENTS]
250 , C: #H = −(%JO/4=1) + (%JO/4=2)
260 , C: #K = (%JO\4=1) − (%JO\4=2)
270 , E: [RETURN]

280 *HEX [DRAW A SMALL HEXAGON]
290 , GR: 6(DRAW 3; TURN 60)
300 , PA:5
310 , E:

SELF-TEST ON CHAPTER 11

1. What number is stored in %T8 when you press the red joystick button?

2. What will this program do?

```
10 *TOP
20 T: %T8
30 J:*TOP
```

3. Complete this program to turn on sound number 1 when the red trigger button is pressed, and be silent when the button is not pressed.

```
10 *TOP
20 ______
30 J:*TOP
```

4. What numbers might you find in %JØ when the joystick is moved?

5. Complete this program so that sound number 1 is turned on when the stick is moved forward; sound number 2 is turned on when the stick is moved backward; sound 4 is turned on when the stick is moved left; sound 8 is turned on when the stick is moved right.

```
10 *TOP
20 ______
30 J:*TOP
```

6. What will this program do?

```
10 *TOP
20 T(%T8): %JØ
30 J:*TOP
```

ANSWERS

1. When the red joystick button is pressed, the number 1 is stored in %T8.

2. The program will type a '1' is the red joystick button is pressed, and will print '0' otherwise.

3. 20 SO: %T8

4. When the joystick is moved you might find any of the numbers 1, 2, 4, 5, 6, 8, 9, 10 in %J∅. If the stick is not moved, you will find 0 there.

5. 20 SO: %J∅

6. The program will print the joystick numbers whenever the red joystick button is pressed.

SUMMARY OF CHAPTER 11

In this chapter you learned:

- that the special number %T8 tells whether the red joystick button is pressed.

- that %T8 equals 0, if the joystick button is not pressed, and equals 1, if the joystick button is pressed

- that %T8 can be used like any other number

- that the special number %J∅ records the position of the joystick

- that the number %J∅ may be used like any other number

- how to use the trigger and the joystick to control the sounds and the turtle

APPENDIX

HOW TO SAVE YOUR PROGRAMS

In this appendix you will learn:

- how to save a program on the ATARI* 410* Cassette Recorder
- how to load a program from the cassette recorder into your computer
- how to save a program on the ATARI* 810* Disk Drive
- how to load a program from the disk drive into your computer

GET DATA CASSETTES

The ATARI* 410* Program Recorder uses cassette tapes similar to those used to record music. The tape has a magnetic surface that stores information. The program recorder requires the very best cassettes to work properly. You can buy high-quality data recording tape at computer stores.

MAKE A PROGRAM

Here is a very short program:

1[RETURN

*Indicates trademark of Atari, Inc. throughout this text.

Now you have a program in the computer. You can store it on the cassette tape.

SET UP YOUR CASSETTE RECORDER

Push the STOP key on your cassette recorder. Up pops the lid. Insert the cassette tape into the space beneath the lid. It only fits one way.

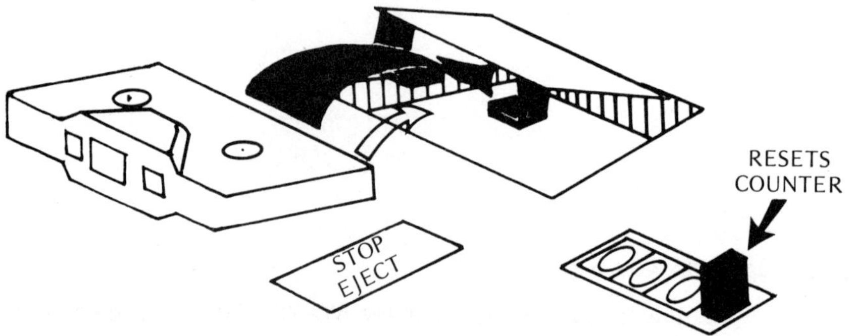

Push down the lid until it locks. Press the REWIND key on the recorder. The tape will rapidly rewind to the beginning of the tape. When the rewind is complete, press the STOP key. Set the tape counter back to 000. Press the small black button next to the program counter.

SAVE YOUR PROGRAM

Type this command:

SAVE:C   [RETURN]

The computer beeps. It is ready to save your program on the cassette recorder. Press down the [RECORD] key and the [PLAY] key at the same time. They stay down. Everything is ready. Press the [RETURN] key on the computer. The tape begins to wind. You can hear the sound of the information passing from the computer to the recorder. You may need to adjust the sound volume on your TV monitor.

When the task is complete, the computer types:

    READY

Now your program is stored on the cassette tape.

Write a short program of your own and save it under some name.

LOAD YOUR PROGRAM

Would you like to check that the program really did get saved on the tape? Here is how you load the information from the tape back into the computer. Press the $\boxed{\text{STOP}}$ key on the cassette recorder. The $\boxed{\text{PLAY}}$ key will pop up. Now press the $\boxed{\text{REWIND}}$ key on the cassette recorder. The tape will rapidly rewind to the beginning of the tape. When the tape is rewound, press the $\boxed{\text{STOP}}$ key on the cassette recorder.
Type this:

    LOAD:C $\boxed{\text{RETURN}}$

The computer beeps twice. Is everything ready? Press down the $\boxed{\text{PLAY}}$ key. It will stay down. Now press the $\boxed{\text{RETURN}}$ key.

The cassette begins to turn and sends information to the computer. You can hear the information load from the recorder into the computer. Adjust the volume of the TV monitor. The computer will type:

    READY

List the program to see if it really loaded into the computer.

THE DISK DRIVE

Start with the disk drive and the computer both turned off. Put the PILOT cartridge in its slot. Turn the disk drive on.

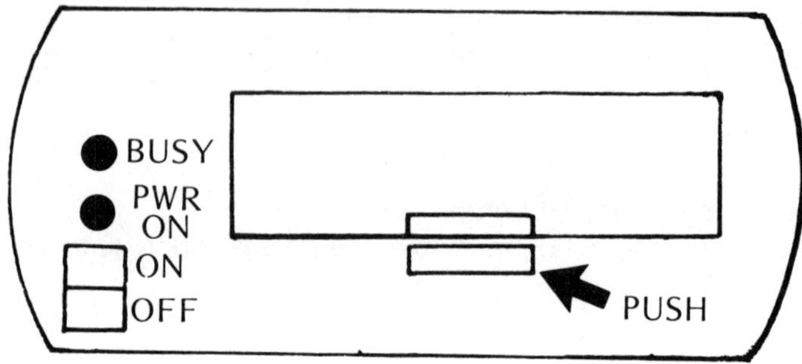

The disk begins to hum. Two red lights are lit. After a few seconds, one light will go out and the drive will stop. Push the long button under the front door of the disk drive. Up pops the door.

THE DOS DISK

The ATARI* 810* Disk Drive uses flexible magnetic disks called floppy disks to store information.

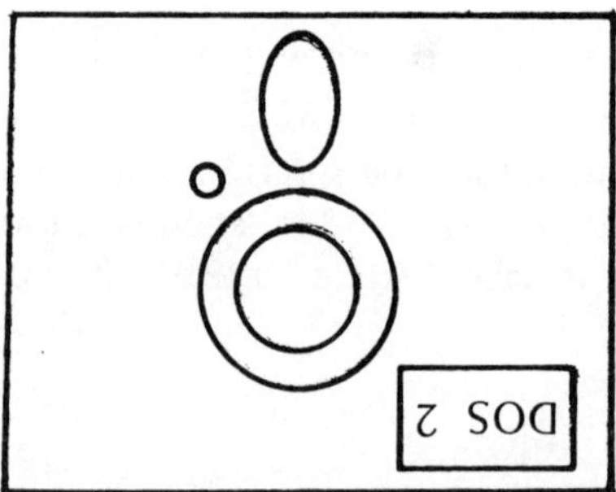

The computer needs some information to manage the disk drive. The information is stored on the disk labeled DOS. Put the DOS disk into the drive. Close the door firmly.

*Indicates trademark of Atari, Inc. throughout this text.

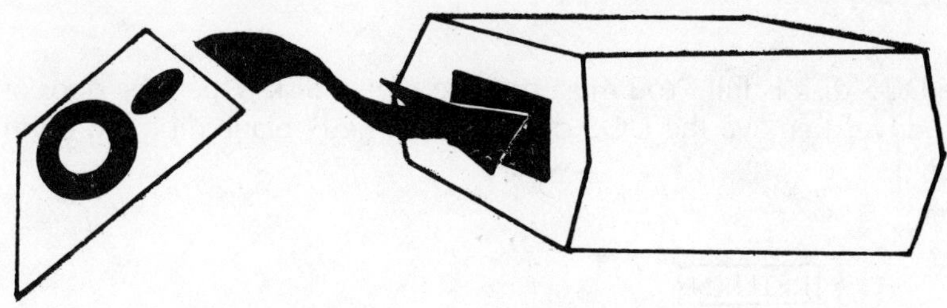

TURN ON THE COMPUTER

When you turn on the computer, the information on the disk is automatically loaded into the computer. When the information has been loaded, the computer will type

READY

To see the program in action, type

DOS   RETURN

You see this menu:

DISK OPERATING SYSTEM II VERSION 2S
COPYRIGHT 1980 ATARI

A.	DISK DIRECTORY	I.	FORMAT DISK
B.	RUN CARTRIDGE	J.	DUPLICATE DISK
C.	COPY FILE	K.	BINARY SAVE
D.	DELETE FILE(S)	L.	BINARY LOAD
E.	RENAME FILE	M.	RUN AT ADDRESS
F.	LOCK FILE	N.	CREATE MEM.SAVE
G.	UNLOCK FILE	O.	DUPLICATE FILE
H.	WRITE DOS FILE		

SELECT ITEM OR RETURN FOR MENU

FORMAT A DISK

The DOS disk is full. You must prepare a new disk. Open the door of the disk drive. Remove the DOS disk. Insert a new, blank disk and close the door.
Type

I   RETURN

This tells the computer to format the disk. The disk begins to click and whirr. Magnetic marks are placed on the disk as reference points for later use. The format process takes a few minutes. When the formatting is complete, the menu again appears.

Type

B   RETURN

This tells the computer to go back to the PILOT cartridge. You see:

READY

WRITE A PROGRAM

You need a program to save. Quick, write a short program:

10 ______
20 ______

SAVE A PROGRAM ONTO THE DISK

To save the program under the name MINE, type this:

SAVE:D:MINE   RETURN

This command saves the program on the disk, under the name MINE. The disk drive spins, and the second red light comes on. The program is saved on the disk.

DOS MENU

Type

DOS   RETURN

You see the Disk Operating System menu.
You can see a list of all programs stored on the disk by typing

A   RETURN

You see the message:

DIRECTORY—SEARCH SPEC, LIST FILE

Press

RETURN

A list of the names of all programs SAVEd appears.

BACK TO PILOT

To get out of the DOS program and back to PILOT, type:

B   RETURN

LOAD A PROGRAM INTO THE COMPUTER

To load the program MINE from the disk into the computer type this:

LOAD:D:MINE   RETURN

The disk spins, and the program is loaded into the computer's memory. You can LIST the program or RUN it.

TURN OFF THE DRIVE

Wait until the drive stops and the top red light goes out. Open the door. Take the disk out of the drive. Put the disk in a safe place, away from dust and magnets. Now it's safe to turn off the disk drive and the computer.

GETTING READY NEXT TIME

The next session will be easier. You have a formatted disk. That job is done for a while. Here are the steps for setting up the disk drive next time:

- Start with everything off.
- Insert the PILOT cartridge.
- Turn on the disk drive; wait till it stops.
- Insert the DOS disk to load the Disk Operating System.
- Turn on the computer.
- When the disk stops, insert the formatted storage disk.

INDEX